Lady Gregory
Interviews and Recollections

Also by E.H. Mikhail

The Social and Cultural Setting of the 1890s
John Galsworthy the Dramatist
Comedy and Tragedy
Sean O'Casey: A Bibliography of Criticism
A Bibliography of Modern Irish Drama 1899–1970
Dissertations on Anglo-Irish Drama: A Bibliography of Studies
1870–1970
The Sting and the Twinkle: Conversations with Sean O'Casey
(*co-editor with John O'Riordan*)
J.M. Synge: A Bibliography of Criticism
J.M. Synge: Interviews and Recollections (*editor*)
English Drama 1900–1950
W.B. Yeats: Interviews and Recollections (two volumes) (*editor*)
Contemporary British Drama 1950–1976

LADY GREGORY

Interviews and Recollections

Edited by

E.H. Mikhail

Selection and editorial matter © E.H. Mikhail 1977

First published 1977 by
THE MACMILLAN PRESS LTD
London and Basingstoke
Associated companies in
Delhi Dublin Hong Kong
Johannesburg Lagos
Melbourne New York
Singapore Tokyo

Typeset by Computacomp (UK) Ltd
Fort William, Scotland
and printed in Great Britain by
BILLING & SONS LTD
Guildford, Worcester and London

British Library Cataloguing in Publication Data

Lady Gregory
  1. Gregory Isabella Augusta, *Lady*
  2. Dramatists – Biography
  I. Mikhail, Edward Halim
  822'.8   PR4728.G5Z

  ISBN 0-333-22327-6

To my wife Isabelle
and my daughters May and Carmen

Contents

Preface   ix

Acknowledgements   xi

INTERVIEWS AND RECOLLECTIONS

A Visit to Coole   *George Moore*   1
Lady Gregory   *George Moore*   8
With Lady Gregory at Coole   *W.B. Yeats*   13
A Visit to Lady Gregory   *Signe Toksvig*   18
Lady Gregory at Rehearsals   *Maire Nic Shiubhlaigh*   27
Kincora   William G. Fay   29
'We Must Teach Them'   *Joseph Holloway*   31
What Lady Gregory Said   32
A Weeding-Out of Words   33
An Exciting Experience   *Walter Starkie*   36
Memories of Lady Gregory   *Wilfrid Scawen Blunt*   39
The Comedy Spirit of Ireland   41
A Lively Discussion over the 'Irish Plays'   46
A Repertory Theatre   48
A Rousing Playboy Riot   52
How Ireland Turned from Politics to Playwriting   54
Lady Gregory Doesn't Mind the Fighting Evenings   60
Lady Gregory: Guiding Genius of the Irish Players   *Chauncey L.*
  Parsons   66
Irish Play Moral   71
Our Trials and Triumphs   *Lady Gregory*   72
Lady Gregory Counselled us Wisely   *Maurice Browne*   75
Lady Gregory and the Abbey Theater   *John Quinn*   77
She Sat Like a Queen   *Walter Starkie*   85

Shanwalla   *Joseph Holloway*   86
Blessed Bridget O'Coole   *Sean O'Casey*   87
Where Wild Swans Nest   *Sean O'Casey*   95
A Visit to Coole Park   *Hallie Flanagan*   106

Index   111

Preface

Lady Gregory was once called by Bernard Shaw 'the greatest living Irishwoman'. W.B. Yeats felt her death profoundly, writing the following day: 'I have lost one who has been to me for nearly forty years my strength and my conscience.' He missed her country home, Coole, which had been 'the only place where I have ever had unbroken health'. Nor did the sorrow grow less; in 1936 he wrote to Lady Dorothy Wellesley: 'I long for quiet; long ago I used to find it at Coole. It was part of the genius of that house.' In addition to being a friend and hostess to all the principal figures of the Irish Renascence, Lady Gregory was a dramatist, co-founder and director of the Abbey Theatre, her country's leading collector of folklore, perfector of the first Anglo-Irish prose idiom fully adapted to literary use, and a staunch fighter for intellectual and artistic freedom.

Yet this great woman was almost forgotten within ten years of her death. There is some autobiographical material in the prefaces to her books and the notes to her plays, but only one biography of her was attempted some thirty years after her death. And even this biography, the author tells us, 'does not pretend to be the documented biography that must be written one day, when all the materials are available'. In the absence of this definitive biography, it is hoped that this collection of interviews and recollections will provide a warm, anecdotal view of an important literary figure.

University of Lethbridge   E.H. MIKHAIL
Alberta, Canada

Acknowledgements

I am grateful to Professor A. Norman Jeffares for his perceptive criticism of the manuscript of this book.

It is also a pleasant duty to record my appreciation to the staff of the University of Lethbridge Library; the British Library, London; the National Library of Ireland, Dublin; Trinity College Library, Dublin; the British Theatre Institute Library, London; and the New York Public Library.

Thanks are due to Miss Bea Ramtej for her patience and skill in typing and preparing the final manuscript; to Mr T.M. Farmiloe of Macmillan for his enthusiasm and encouragement; to Miss Julia Brittain and her colleagues of the same firm for their help in seeing the book through the press; and to Mr John Prince for compiling the index.

The editor and publishers wish to thank the following who have kindly given permission for the use of copyright material:

The Boston Globe for the extract 'A Lively Discussion over the "Irish Plays" ' from the *Sunday Post*, 8 Oct 1911.

Boston Herald American for the extract 'The Comedy Spirit of Ireland' from the *Sunday Herald*, 1 Oct 1911 (Magazine section).

Coward, McCann & Geoghegan, Inc., for the extract 'A Visit to Coole Park' from *Shifting Scenes of the Modern European Theatre*, edited by Hallie Flanagan (1928).

James Duffy & Co. Ltd for the extract 'Lady Gregory at Rehearsals' from *The Splendid Years* by Maire Nic Shiubhlaigh (1955).

Victor Gollancz Ltd for the extract 'Lady Gregory Counselled Us Wisely' from *Too Late to Lament; An Autobiography* by Maurice Browne.

Hutchinson Publishing Group Ltd for the extract from 'The Fays of the Abbey Theatre' by William G. Fay (1935).

Independent Newspapers Ltd for the extracts 'What Lady Gregory said' from the *Evening Telegraph* (Dublin), 29 Jan 1907, and 'A Weeding-Out of Words' from *The Playboy has a Quieter Time at the Abbey*, *Evening Herald* (Dublin), 1 Feb 1907.

Macmillan Publishing Company Inc., for the extracts 'Blessed Bridget O'Coole' and 'Where Wild Swans Nest' from *Inishfallen, Fare*

A Visit to Coole*

GEORGE MOORE

After long ringing the maidservant opened the door[1] and told me that Lady Gregory had gone to church with her niece; Mr Yeats was composing.[2] Would I take a seat in the drawing-room and wait till he was finished? He must have heard the wheels of the car coming round the gravel sweep, for he was in the room before the servant left it—enthusiastic, though a little weary. He had written five lines and a half, and a pause between one's rhymes is an excellent thing, he said. One could not but admire him, for even in early morning he was convinced of the importance of literature in our national life. He is nearly as tall as a Dublin policeman, and preaching literature he stood on the hearthrug, his feet set close together. Lifting his arms above his head (the very movement that Raphael gives to Paul when preaching at Athens), he said what he wanted to do was to gather up a great mass of speech. It did not seem to me clear why he should be at pains to gather up a great mass of speech to write so exiguous a thing as *The Shadowy Waters*;[3] but we live in our desires rather than in our achievements, and Yeats talked on, telling me that he was experimenting, and did not know whether his play would come out in rhyme or in blank verse; he was experimenting. He could write blank verse almost as easily as prose, and therefore feared it; some obstacle, some dam was necessary. It seemed a pity to interrupt him, but I was interested to hear if he were going to accept my end, and allow the lady to drift southward, drinking yellow ale with the sailors, while the hero sought salvation alone in the North. He flowed out into a torrent of argument and explanation, very ingenious, but impossible to follow. Phrase after phrase rose and turned and went out like a wreath of smoke, and when the last was spoken and the idea it had borne had vanished, I asked him if he knew the legend of Diarmuid[4] and Grania.[5] He began to tell it to me in its many variants, surprising me with unexpected dramatic situations, at first sight contradictory and incoherent, but on closer scrutiny revealing a psychology in germ which it would interest me to unfold. A wonderful hour of literature that was, flowering into a resolution to

*Extracted from *Ave* (London: William Heinemann, 1911).

write an heroic play together.[6] As we sat looking at each other in silence, Lady Gregory returned from church.

She came into the room quickly, with a welcoming smile on her face, and I set her down here as I see her: a middle-aged woman, agreeable to look upon, perhaps for her broad, handsome, intellectual brow enframed in iron-grey hair. The brown, wide-open eyes are often lifted in looks of appeal and inquiry, and a natural wish to sympathise softens her voice till it whines. It modulated, however, very pleasantly as she yielded her attention to Yeats, who insisted on telling her how two beings so different as myself and Whelan[7] had suddenly become united in a conspiracy to deceive Edward,[8] Whelan because he could not believe in the efficacy of a Mass performed by an anti-Parnellite,[9] and I because—Yeats hesitated for a sufficient reason, deciding suddenly that I had objected to hear Mass in Gort[10] because there was no one in the church who had read Villiers de l'Isle–Adam[11] except myself; and he seemed so much amused that the thought suddenly crossed my mind that perhaps the *cocasseries*[12] of Connaught[13] were more natural to him than the heroic moods which he believed himself called upon to interpret. His literature is one thing and his conversation is another, divided irreparably. Is this right? Lady Gregory chattered on, telling stories faintly farcical, amusing to those who knew the neighbourhood, but rather wearisome for one who didn't, and I was waiting for an opportunity to tell her that an heroic drama was going to be written on the subject of Diarmuid and Grania.

When my lips broke the news, a cloud gathered in her eyes, and she admitted that she thought it would be hardly wise for Yeats to undertake any further work at present;[14] and later in the afternoon she took me into her confidence, telling me that Yeats came to Coole every summer because it was necessary to get him away from the distractions of London, not so much from social as from the intellectual distractions that Arthur Symons[15] had inaugurated. *The Savoy*[16] rose up in my mind with its translations from Villiers de l'Isle–Adam, Verlaine,[17] and Maeterlinck;[18] and I agreed with her that alien influences were a great danger to the artist. All Yeats's early poems, she broke in, were written in Sligo,[19] and among them were twenty beautiful lyrics and Ireland's one great poem, *The Wanderings of Usheen*[20]—all these had come straight out of the landscape and the people he had known from boyhood.

For seven years we have been waiting for a new book from him; ever since *The Countess Cathleen*[21] we have been reading the publisher's autumn announcement of *The Wind among the Reeds*.[22] The volume was finished here last year; it would never have been finished if I had not asked him to Coole; and though we live in an ungrateful world, I think somebody will throw a kind word after me some day, if for nothing else, for *The Wind among the Reeds*.

I looked round, thinking that perhaps life at Coole was arranged primarily to give him an opportunity of writing poems. As if she had read my thoughts, Lady Gregory led me into the back drawing-room, and showed me the table at which he wrote, and I admired the clean pens, the fresh ink, and the spotless blotter; these were her special care every morning. I foresaw the strait sofa lying across the window, valued in some future time because the poet had reclined upon it between his rhymes. Ah me! the creeper that rustles an accompaniment to his melodies in the pane will awaken again, year after year, but one year it will awaken in vain.... My eyes thanked Lady Gregory for her devotion to literature. Instead of writing novels she had released the poet from the quern of daily journalism, and anxious that she should understand my appreciation of her, I spoke of the thirty-six wild swans that had risen out of the lake while Yeats and I wandered all through the long evening seeking a new composition for *The Shadowy Waters*.

She did not answer me, and I followed her in silence back to the front room and sat listening to her while she told me that it was because she wanted poems from him that she looked askance at our project to write a play together on the subject of Diarmuid and Grania. It was not that the subject was unsuited to his genius, but she thought it should be written by him alone; the best of neither would transpire in collaboration, and she lamented that it were useless to save him from the intellectual temptations of Symons if he were to be tossed into more subtle ones. She laughed, as is her way when she cozens, and reminded me that we were of different temperaments and had arisen out of different literary traditions.

Mayo[23] went to Montmartre,[24] and Sligo turned into Fleet Street.[25]

Suspicious in her cleverness, my remark did not altogether please her, and she said something about a man of genius and a man of talent coming together, speaking quickly under her breath, so that her scratch would escape notice at the time; and we were talking of our responsibilities towards genius when the door opened and Yeats came into the room.

He entered somewhat diffidently, I thought, with an invitation to me to go for a walk. Lady Gregory was appeased with the news that he had written five and a half lines that morning, and a promise that he would be back at six, and would do a little more writing before dinner. As he went away he told me that he might attain his maximum of nine lines that evening, if he succeeded in finishing the broken line. But S must never meet S; for his sake was inadmissible, and while seeking how he might avoid such a terrifying cacophony we tramped down wet roads and climbed over low walls into scant fields, finding the ruined castle we were in search of at the end of a long boreen among tall, wet grasses. The walls were intact and the stair, and from the top we stood watching the mist drifting across the grey country, Yeats telling how the wine had been drugged at Tara,[26] myself thinking how natural it was that Lady Gregory should look upon me as a danger to Yeats's genius. As we descended the slippery stair an argument began in my head whereby our project of collaboration might be defended. Next time I went to Coole I would say to Lady Gregory: You see, Yeats came to me with *The Shadowy Waters* because he had entangled the plot and introduced all his ideas into it, and you will admit that the plot had to be disentangled? To conciliate her completely I would say that while Yeats was rewriting *The Shadowy Waters* I would spend my time writing an act about the many adventures that befell Diarmuid and Grania as they fled before Finn.[27] Yeats had told me these adventures in the ruined castle; I had given to them all the attention that I could spare from Lady Gregory, who, I was thinking, might admit my help in the arrangement of some incidents in *The Shadowy Waters,* but would always regard our collaboration in *Diarmuid and Grania* with hostility. But for this partiality it seemed to me I could not blame her, so well had she put her case when she said that her fear was that my influence might break up the mould of his mind.

The car waited for me at the end of the boreen, and before starting I tried to persuade Yeats to come to Tillyra[28] with me, but he said he could not leave Lady Gregory alone, and before we parted I learnt that she read to him every evening. Last summer it was *War and Peace,* and this summer she was reading Spenser's *Faerie Queene,* for he was going to publish a selection[29] and must get back to Coole for the seventh canto.

Good-bye, and springing up on the car, I was driven by Whelan into the mist, thinking Yeats the most fortunate amongst us, he having discovered among all others that one who, by instinctive sympathy, understood the capacity of his mind, and could evoke it, and who never wearied of it, whether it came to her in elaborately wrought stanzas or in the form of some simple confession, the mood of last night related as they crossed the sward after breakfast. As the moon is more interested in the earth than in any other thing, there is always some woman more interested in a man's mind than in anything else, and willing to follow it sentence by sentence. A great deal of Yeats's work must come to her in fragments—a line and a half, two lines—and these she faithfully copies on her typewriter, and even those that his ultimate taste has rejected are treasured up, and perhaps will one day appear in a stately variorum edition.

Well she may say that the future will owe her something, and my thoughts moved back to the first time I saw her some twenty-five years ago.[30] She was then a young woman, very earnest, who divided her hair in the middle and wore it smooth on either side of a broad and handsome brow. Her eyes were always full of questions, and her

Protestant high-school air became her greatly and estranged me from her.

In her drawing-room were to be met men of assured reputation in literature and politics, and there was always the best reading of the time upon her tables. There was nothing, however, in her conversation to suggest literary faculty, and it was a surprise to me to hear one day that she had written a pamphlet in defence of Arabi Pasha, an Egyptian rebel.[31] Some years after she edited her husband's memoirs,[32] and did the work well. So at core she must have been always literary, but early circumstances had not proved favourable to the development of her gift, and it languished till she met Yeats. He could not have been long at Coole before he began to draw her attention to the beauty of the literature that rises among the hills and bubbles irresponsibly, and set her going from cabin to cabin taking down stories, and encouraged her to learn the original language of the country, so that they might add to the Irish idiom which the peasant had already translated into English, making in this way a language for themselves.

Yeats could only acquire the idiom by the help of Lady Gregory, for although he loves the dialect and detests the defaced idiom which we speak in our streets and parlours, he has little aptitude to learn that of the boreen and the market-place. She put her aptitude at his service, and translated portions of Cathleen ni Houlihan[33] into Kiltartan (Kiltartan is the village in which she collects the dialect); and she worked it into the revised version of the stories from The Secret Rose,[34] published by the Dun Emer Press, and thinking how happy their lives must be at Coole, implicated in literary partnership, my heart went out towards her in a sudden sympathy. She has been wise all her life through, I said; she knew him to be her need at once, and she never hesitated ... yet she knew me before she knew him.

NOTES

George Moore (1852–1933), Irish novelist and man of letters. As an innovator in fiction he does not now seem so important as he once did, but *Esther Waters* (1894) will always deserve readers, and in an autobiographical trilogy, *Hail and Farewell* (1911–14), he gained the rare achievement of finding an original prose form of his own outside the novel. In Paris Moore became friendly with the avant-garde Impressionist group vividly described in *Reminiscences of the Impressionist Painters* (1906). Another account of the years in Paris, in which he introduced the younger generation in England to his version of *fin de siècle* decadence, was his first autobiography *Confessions of a Young Man* (1888). Moore moved to Dublin, where he contributed notably to the planning of the Irish Literary Theatre, but Irish politics and clericalism sent him back to England in 1911. While he lived in Dublin he produced a volume of fine short stories about Ireland, *The Untilled Field* (1903), and an experimental novel, *The Lake* (1905), where he developed the 'melodic line'.

1. Of Lady Gregory's country house, Coole Park, Gort, County Galway.
2. When W.B. Yeats met Lady Gregory in 1896, she asked him to visit Coole the

following summer, and this old house was to become almost a second home to him through many years of his life. Yeats's first poem on Coole was 'In the Seven Woods'.

3. *The Shadowy Waters* had its première at the Molesworth Hall, Dublin on 14 January 1904.

4. Diarmaid or Diarmuid O'Duibhne, Irish hero of the Fianna in love-story with Princess Grainne, irresistible to women by reason of the love-spot on his forehead. Jealous Finn MacCoul (to whome Grainne had been betrothed) tricked him into walking on a boar's skin where a bristle fatally poisoned his heel.

5. Grania or Grainne, daughter of King Cormac. At a feast she put all to slumber except Diarmuid whom she bound by charm to flee with her. In flight Aengus gave her a mantle of invisibility to escape pursuit by Finn MacCoul.

6. Yeats and George Moore collaborated on *Diarmuid and Grania*, which had its first production by the Irish Literary Theatre at the Gaiety Theatre, Dublin, on 21 October 1901. Lady Gregory had her share in the play too, besides receiving with apparent meekness Yeats's suggestion that Moore should first write it in French, and she then translate it into her 'speech of the people', which they had not yet begun to call 'Kiltartan'. In *Our Irish Theatre* Lady Gregory summarises her share thus: 'I began by writing bits of dialogue, when wanted. Mr Yeats used to dictate parts of *Diarmuid and Grania* to me, and I would suggest a sentence here and there.' Moore having failed as a dramatic collaborator, Yeats turned to Lady Gregory.

7. The coachman.

8. Edward Martyn (1859–1923) who, by financial support and his two best plays *The Heather Field* (1899) and *Maeve* (1900), did much to set the Irish Dramatic Movement on its feet. It was in 1899 that W.B. Yeats, Edward Martyn, George Moore, and Lady Gregory founded the Irish Literary Theatre in Dublin under the auspices of the National Literary Society created in 1891. See Sister Marie-Therese Courtney, *Edward Martyn and the Irish Theatre* (New York: Vantage Press, 1956.)

9. Charles Stuart Parnell (1846–91), nationalist leader of the struggle for Irish Home Rule in the late nineteenth century. 'With the passing away of Parnell's long dominance, his necessary discipline,' Lady Gregory says in her *Hugh Lane's Life and Achievement,* 'there had come a setting loose of the mind, of the imagination, that had for so long dwelt upon some battle at Westminster or some disputed farm.'

10. Lady Gregory's county town.

11. Villiers de l'Isle-Adam (1838–89), French writer and the reputed originator of the Symbolist school in French literature. See A.M. Killen, 'Some French Influences in the Works of W.B. Yeats at the End of the Nineteenth Century', *Comparative Literature Studies,* VIII (1942) 1–8.

12. Oddities; antics.

13. Connaught, also spelled Connact, one of the five ancient kingdoms or provinces of Ireland, lies in the western and northwestern areas of the island and comprises the modern counties of Mayo, Sligo, Leitrim, Galway and Roscommon.

14. Doubtless Moore's story explains Lady Gregory's deciding that if Yeats required, as he seemed to do, a dramatic collaborator, then in future it had better be herself.

15. Arthur Symons (1865–1945), poet and critic, the first English champion of the French Symbolist poets, who sought to convey impressions by suggestion rather than direct statement.

16. In 1896, Arthur Symons became editor of a new magazine, *The Savoy,* with Aubrey Beardsley as art editor.

17. Paul Verlaine (1844–96), among the most gifted of the French lyric poets of the later nineteenth century.

18. Maurice Maeterlinck (1862–1949), Symbolist poet and playwright whose rhythmic prose dramas are the outstanding works of the Symbolist theatre. The most famous Belgian writer of his day, he wrote in French, and, for the most part, it was to French literary movements that he looked for inspiration.

19. W.B. Yeat's home county.

20. W.B. Yeats, *The Wanderings of Oisin and Other Poems* (London: Kegan Paul, Trench, 1889).

21. W.B. Yeats, *The Countess Kathleen and Various Legends and Lyrics* (London: T. Fisher Unwin, 1891).

22. W.B. Yeats, *The Wind among the Reeds* (London: Elkin Mathews, 1899).

23. George Moore's home county.

24. A northern district of Paris on the right bank of the River Seine, occupying the highest point in Paris, long a favourite residential area for artists.

25. Home of Britain's national newspapers.

26. Low hill (about 507 feet) in County Meath occupying an important place in Irish Legend and history.

27. Fionn MacCumhal (Finn MacCoul). Variants Finn, Find. Same as Fingal, identified in the Fenian cycle of legends as the Fianna's champion of Ireland, superhuman in size, strength, speed, and prowess.

28. Tullira Castle, Edward Martyn's country residence, five miles away from Coole. Tullira and Coole were on very good terms. Later on, Martyn grew jealous of Lady Gregory, and felt that she had stolen his friends. But it was his own increasing eccentricity, after his mother's death, that made Tullira a less pleasant house to stay in than Coole.

29. *Poems of Spenser*. Selected with an Introduction by W.B. Yeats (Edinburgh: T.C. & E.C. Jack, 1906).

30. The picture which Moore has left of Lady Gregory in *Ave* is unsympathetic but probably not altogether unjust. There is a rueful description of her young-married self in the *Journals* of her later life. In *Vale* (having in the meantime quarrelled with Yeats), Moore strengthens the unsympathetic element.

31. The winter of 1881–2, spent by the Gregorys in Egypt, was an important one for Augusta, for it was then that, as she puts it, she 'made her education in politics'. The leaders of the English colony in Cairo were the Sussex poet and landowner Wilfrid Scawen Blunt and his wife Lady Anne, granddaughter of Byron. Blunt was a great taker-up of causes. His current cause when he met the Gregorys was that of Arabi Bey, an Egyptian officer who had risen by his own abilities from the peasant class, and was leading a successful and bloodless revolt against the corruption and incompetence of the Turkish rule. The British authorities regarded him with suspicion, but Blunt had no difficulty in converting the Gregorys to his view that this was a genuine nationalist movement, deserving of support. Sir William Gregory proceeded to write a series of letters to *The Times,* and later in 1882 Lady Gregory wrote a 5000-word pamphlet, *Arabi and His Household,* which sold for twopence, and was her first published work.

32. *Autobiography of Sir William Gregory,* ed. Lady Gregory (London: Murray, 1894).

33. *Cathleen ni Houlihan,* by W.B. Yeats, was first performed by the Irish National Society at St Teresa's Hall, Dublin, on 2 April 1902.

34. W.B. Yeats, *The Secret Rose* (London: Lawrence & Bullen, 1897).

Lady Gregory*

GEORGE MOORE

Lady Gregory is a Persse, and the Persses are an ancient Galway family; the best-known branch is Moyaude, for it was at Moyaude that Burton Persse bred and hunted the Galway Blazers for over thirty years ... till his death. Moyaude has passed away, but Roxburgh continues, never having indulged in either horses or hounds, a worthy but undistinguished family in love, in war, or in politics, never having indulged in anything except a taste for Bible reading in cottages. A staunch Protestant family, if nothing else, the Roxborough Persses certainly are. Mrs. Shaw Taylor [sic][1] is Lady Gregory's sister, and both were ardent soul-gatherers in the days gone by; but Augusta abandoned missionary work when she married, and we like to think of sir William[2] saying to his bride, as he brought her home in the carriage to Coole, 'Augusta, if you have made no converts, you have at least shaken the faith of thousands. The ground at Roxburgh has been cleared for the sowing, but Kiltartan can wait.' And the bride may have agreed to accept her husband's authority, for had she not promised to love, honour, and obey? However this may be, the Gospels were not read by Lady Gregory round Kiltartan. I should like to fill in a page or two about her married life, but though we know our neighbours very well in one direction, in another there is nothing that we know less than our neighbours, and Lady Gregory has never been for me a very real person. I imagine her without a mother, or father, or sisters, or brothers, sans attache.[3] It is difficult to believe, but it is nevertheless true, that fearing a too flagrant mistake, I had to ask a friend the other day if I were right in supposing that Mrs. Shaw Taylor was Lady Gregory's sister, an absurd question truly, for Mrs. Shaw Taylor's house (I have forgotten its name)[4] is within a mile of Tillyra, and I must have been there many times. We may cultivate our memories in one direction, but by so doing we curtail them in another, and documentary evidence is not of my style. I like to write of Lady Gregory from the evening that Edward drove me over to Coole, the night of the dinner-party. There is in Ave a portrait of her as I saw her

*Extracted from Vale (London: William Heinemann, 1914).

that night, a slim young woman of medium height and slight figure; her hair, parted in the middle, was brushed in wide bands about a brow which even at that time was intellectual. The phrase used in *Ave*, if my memory does not deceive me, was 'high and cultured'; I think I said that she wore a high-school air, and the phrase expresses the idea she conveyed to me—an air of mixed timidity and restrained anxiety to say or do nothing that would jar. On the whole it was pleasant to pass from her to Sir William, who was more at his ease, more natural. He spoke to me affably about a Velasquez[5] in the National Gallery, which was not a Velasquez; it is now set down as a Zurbaran[6] but the last attribution does not convince me any more than the first. He wore the Lord Palmerston[7] air, it was the air of that generation, but he did not wear it nearly so well as my father.

These two men were of the same generation and their interests were the same; both were travelled men; Sir William's travels were not so original as my father's, and the race-horses that he kept were not so fast, and his politics were not so definite; he was more of an opportunist than my father, more careful and cautious, and therefore less interesting. Galway has not produced so many interesting men as Mayo; its pastures are richer, but its men are thinner in intellect. But if we are considering Lady Gregory's rise in the world, we must admit that she owes a great deal to her husband. He took her to London, and she enjoyed at least one season in a tall house in the little enclosure known as St. George's Place; and there met a number of eminent men whose books and conversation were in harmony with her conception of life, still somewhat formal. One afternoon Lecky[8] the historian left her drawing-room as I entered it, and I remember the look of pleasure on her face when she mentioned the name of her visitor, and her pleasure did not end with Lecky, for a few minutes after Edwin Arnold,[9] the poet of *The Light of Asia,* was announced. She would like to have had him all to herself, and I think that she thought my conversation a little ill-advised when I spoke to Sir Edwin of a book lately published on the subject of Buddhism, and asked him what book was the best to read on this subject. He did not answer my question directly, but very soon he was telling Lady Gregory that he had just received a letter from India from a distinguished Buddhist who had read *The Light of Asia* and could find no fault in it; the Buddhist doctrine as related by him had been related faultlessly. And with this little anecdote Sir Edwin thought my question sufficiently answered. The conversation turned on the coloured races, and I remember Sir Edwin's words: 'The world will not be perfect,' he said, 'until we get the black notes into the gamut.' A pretty bit of telegraphese which pleased Lady Gregory; and when Sir Edwin rose to go she produced a fan and asked him to write his name upon one of the sticks.[10] But she did not ask me to write my name, though at that time I had written not only *A Modern Lover,* but also *A Mummer's Wife*,[11] and I left the house feeling for the first time that the world I lived in was not so profound as I had imagined it to be. If I remember the circumstances quite rightly, Sir William came into the room just as I was leaving it, and she showed him the fan; he looked a little distressed at her want of tact, and it was some years afterwards that I heard, and not without surprise, that she had shown some literary ability in the editing of his *Memoirs.* The publication of these *Memoirs* was a great day for Roxburgh, and a great day for Ireland it was when she drove over to Tillyra.

I was not present at the time, but from Edward's account of the meeting she seems to have recognised her need in Yeats at once, foreseeing, dimly, of course, but foreseeing that he would help her out of conventions and prejudices, and give her wings to soar in the free air of ideas and instincts. She was manifestly captured by his genius, and seemed to dread that the inspiration the hills of Sligo had nourished might wither in the Temple where he used to spend long months with his friend Arthur Symons. He had finished all his best work at the time, the work whereby he will live; *The Countess Cathleen* had not long been written, and he was dreaming the poem of *The Shadowy Waters,* and where could he dream more fortunately than by the lake at Coole? The wild swans[12] gather here, and every summer he returned to Coole to write *The Shadowy Waters,* writing under her tutelage and she serving him as amanuensis, collecting the different versions, &c.

So much of the literary history of this time was written in *Ave,* but what has not been written, or only hinted at, is the interdependence of these two minds. It was he, no doubt, who suggested to her the writing of the Cuchulain[13] legends. It must have been so, for he had long been dreaming an epic poem to be called *Cuchulain*; but feeling himself unable for so long a task, he entrusted it to Lady Gregory, and led her from cabin to cabin in search of a style, and they returned to Coole ruminating the beautiful language of the peasants and the masterpiece quickening in it, Yeats a little sad, but by no means envious towards Lady Gregory, and sad, if at all, that his own stories in the volume entitled *The Secret Rose* were not written in living speech. It is pleasant to think that, as he opened the park gates for her to pass through, the thought glided into his mind that perhaps in some subsequent edition she might help him with the translation. But the moment was for the consideration of a difficulty that had arisen suddenly. The legends of Cuchulain are written in a very remote language, bearing little likeness to the modern Irish which Lady Gregory had learnt in common with everybody connected with the Irish Literary Movement, Yeats and myself excepted. A dictionary of the ancient language exists, and it is easy to look out a word; but a knowledge of early or middle Irish is only obtained gradually after years of study; Lady Gregory confesses herself in her preface to be no scholar, and that she pieced together her text from various French and German translations. This method recommends itself to Yeats, who says in his preface that by collating the various versions of the same tale and taking the best bits out of each, the stories are now told perfectly for the first time, a singular view for a critic of Yeats's understanding to hold, a strange theory to advocate, the strangest, we do not hesitate to say, that has ever been put forward by so distinguished a poet and critic as Yeats. He was a severer critic the day that he threw out Edward's play[14] with so much indignity in Tillyra. He was then a monk of literature, an inquisitor, a Torquemada,[15] but in this preface he bows to Lady Gregory's taste as if she were the tale-teller that the world had been waiting for, one whose art exceeded that of Balzac[16] or Turgenev,[17] for neither would have claimed the right to refashion the old legends in accordance with his own taste or the taste of his neighbourhood. 'I left out a good deal,' Lady Gregory writes in her preface, 'I thought you would not care about.' The 'you' refers to the people of Kiltartan, to whom Lady Gregory dedicates her book. It seems to me that Balzac and Turgenev would have taken a different view as to the duty of a modern writer to the old legends; both would have said, 'It is never justifiable to alter a legend; it has come down to us because it contains some precious message, and the message the legend carries will be lost or worsened if the story be altered or mutilated or deformed.' 'And who am I,' Balzac would have said, 'that I should alter a message that has come down from a far-off time, a message often enfolded in the tale so secretly that it is all things to all men? My province,' he would have said, 'is not to alter the story, but to interpret it,' and we have not to listen very intently to hear him say, 'Not only I may, I must interpret.' There can be little doubt that Yeats is often injudicious in his noble preface, and he exposes Lady Gregory to ciritcism when he depreciates the translation from which Lady Gregory said she worked. She might have written 'which I quote,' for she follows Kuno Meyer's[18] translation of the *Wooing of Emer* sentence by sentence, and it is our puzzle to discover how Kuno Meyer's English is worthless when he signs it, and beautiful when Lady Gregory quotes it. 'A clear case of literary transubstantiation,' I said, speaking of the miracle to a friend who happened to be a Roman Catholic, and she gave me the definition of the catechism; the substance is the same, but the incident is different. Or it may have been that the incident is the same and the substance is different; one cannot ever be sure that one remembers theology correctly. A little examination, however, of Lady Gregory's text enabled us to dismiss the theological aspect as untenable. Here and there we find she has altered the words; Kuno Meyer's title is *The Wooing of Emer,* Lady Gregory has changed it to *The Courting of Emer* (she is writing living speech); and if Kuno Meyer wrote that Emer[19] received Cuchulain in her bower, Lady Gregory, for the same reason, would certainly change it to she asked him into her 'parlour.' The word 'lawn' in the sentence 'and as the young girls were sitting together on their bench on the lawn they heard coming towards them a clattering of hooves, the creaking of a chariot, the grating of wheels,' belongs to Lady Gregory; of that I am so sure that it would be needless for me to refer to Kuno Meyer's version of the legend.

NOTES

1. Mrs Elizabeth Shawe-Taylor.

2. When Lady Gregory was twenty-seven, and hopes of finding a *parti* for her had probably been abandoned, her eldest brother, Richard, fell ill. Doctors recommended the south of France, and Mrs Persse, his mother, took him to Nice, taking Augusta also to share in the nursing. At Nice they met their neighbour Sir William Gregory of Coole, recently retired from the governorship of Ceylon. Augusta Persse and Sir William Gregory were married on 4 March 1880 at St Matthias, Dublin.

3. Unattached.

4. Castle Taylor.

5. Diego Velázquez (1599–1660), major Spanish painter of the seventeenth century, acknowledged as one of the giants of Western art.

6. Francisco de Zurbarán (1598–1664), important painter of the Spanish Baroque, especially noted as a painter of religious subjects.

7. Lord Palmerston (1784–1865), Whig-Liberal statesman whose long career, including more than thirty years as British Foreign Secretary or Prime Minister, made him a permanent embodiment of British nationalism.

8. William Edward Hartpole Lecky (1838–1903), historian of rationalism and European morals. His eight-volume *History of England in the Eighteenth Century* (1878–90) is a classic study of Georgian England.

9. Sir Edwin Arnold (1832–1904), English poet and scholar, best known as the author of *The Light of Asia* (1879), an epic poem that tells, in elaborate language, of the life and teachings of Buddha.

10. Lady Gregory in the course of her life filled two fans with autographs of celebrities. For details of the signatures see Elizabeth Coxhead, *Lady Gregory; A Literary Portrait,* 2nd ed., revised and enlarged (London: Secker & Warburg, 1966) p. 31.

11. George Moore's first novels, *A Modern Lover* (1883) and *A Mummer's Wife* (1885), introduced to the Victorian novel a new note of French Naturalism, and he later adopted the realistic techniques of such writers as Flaubert and Balzac.

12. Yeats wrote a poem entitled 'The Wild Swans at Coole'.

13. Cuchulainn or Cuchulinn, reputed rebirth-son of Lug the Sun-god by Goddess Dectire. Champion hero of a cycle of myths, who at the age of seventeen defended Ulster single-handed for four months.

14. Edward Martyn's political satire *The Tale of a Town.* Martyn handed over the play to Moore, who called in Yeats to help him with the political subject-matter. Yeats was invited to Tullira Castle, and instead of sharing Moore's concern for the disconsolate Martyn sitting alone in the tower of the castle, merely said, 'We couldn't produce such a play as that.' *The Tale of a Town* became *The Bending of the Bough* and Moore appeared as its sole author.

15. Tomás de Torquemada (1420–98), first grand inquisitor in Spain, whose name

has become synonymous with the Inquisition's horror, religious bigotry, and cruel fanaticism.

16. Honoré de Balzac (1799–1850), universally recognised as a genius in the novel, converted what had been styled 'romance' into a convincing record of human experience. His vast lifework was arranged under the title *La Comédie humaine (The Human Comedy)*, in which he claimed at once to be a philosopher explaining man to himself, a historian or 'secretary' of society, and a sociologist and psychologist.

17. Ivan Turgenev (1818–83), Russian novelist, poet, and playwright whose writings evince deep concern for the future of his native land.

18. Kuno Meyer (1858–1919), German scholar of the Celtic languages and editor whose translations made him the chief interpreter of early Irish literature for English and German readers. In 1903 he established the School of Irish Learning, Dublin, and the following year founded its journal *Erin* [Ireland].

19. Devoted wife of Cuchulain.

With Lady Gregory at Coole*

W.B. YEATS

A couple of weeks after my vision,[1] Lady Gregory, whom I had met once in London for a few minutes, drove over to Tulira, and after Symons's return to London I stayed at her house. When I saw her great woods on the edge of a lake, I remembered the saying about avoiding woods and living near the water. Had this new friend come because of my invocation, or had the saying been but prevision and my invocation no act of will, but prevision also? Were those unintelligible words—'avoid woods because they concentrate the solar ray'—but a dream-confusion, an attempt to explain symbolically an actual juxtaposition of wood and water? I could not say nor can I now. I was in poor health, the strain of youth had been greater than it commonly is, even with imaginative men, who must always, I think, find youth bitter, and I had lost myself besides, as I had done periodically for years, upon Hodos Chameliontos. The first time was in my eighteenth or nineteenth year, when I tried to create a more multitudinous dramatic form, and now I had got there through a novel[2] that I could neither write nor cease to write which had Hodos Chameliontos for its theme. My chief person was to see all the modern visionary sects pass before his bewildered eyes, as Flaubert's[3] Saint Anthony saw the Christian sects,[4] and I was as helpless to create artistic, as my chief person to create philosophic,

*Extracted from *The Trembling of the Veil* (London: T. Werner Laurie, 1922).

order. It was not that I do not love order, or that I lack capacity for it, but that—and not in the arts and in thought only—I outrun my strength. It is not so much that I choose too many elements, as that the possible unities themselves seem without number, like those angels that, in Henry More's[5] paraphrase of the schoolman's problem, dance spurred and booted upon the point of a needle. Perhaps fifty years ago I had been in less trouble, but what can one do when the age itself has come to Hodos Chameliontos?

Lady Gregory, seeing that I was ill, brought me from cottage to cottage to gather folk-belief,[6] tales of the faeries, and the like, and wrote down herself what we had gathered, considering that this work, in which one let others talk, and walked about the fields so much, would lie, to use a country phrase, 'very light upon the mind'. She asked me to return there the next year, and for years to come I was to spend my summers at her house. When I was in good health again, I found myself indolent, partly perhaps because I was affrighted by that impossible novel, and asked her to send me to my work every day at eleven, and at some other hour to my letters, rating me with idleness if need be, and I doubt if I should have done much with my life but for her firmness and her care.[7] After a time, though not very quickly, I recovered tolerable industry, though it has only been of late years that I have found it possible to face an hour's verse without a preliminary struggle and much putting off.

Certain woods at Sligo, the woods above Dooney Rock[8] and those above the waterfall at Ben Bulben,[9] though I shall never perhaps walk there again, are so deep in my affections that I dream about them at night; and yet the woods at Coole,[10] though they do not come into my dream, are so much more knitted to my thought that when I am dead they will have, I am persuaded, my longest visit. When we are dead, according to my belief, we live our lives backward for certain number of years, treading the paths that we have trodden, growing young again, even childish again, till some attain an innocence that is no longer a mere accident of nature, but the human intellect's crowning achievement. It was at Coole that the first few simple thoughts that now, grown complex through their contact with other thoughts, explain the world, came to me from beyond my own mind. I practised meditations, and these, as I think, so affected my sleep that I began to have dreams that differed from ordinary dreams in seeming to take place amid brilliant light, and by their invariable coherence, and certain half-dreams, if I can call them so, between sleep and waking. I have noticed that such experiences come to me most often amid distraction, at some time that seems of all times the least fitting, as though it were necessary for the exterior mind to be engaged elsewhere, and it was during 1897 and 1898, when I was always just arriving from or just setting out to some political meeting, that the first dreams came. I was crossing a little stream near Inchy Wood and actually in the middle of a stride from bank to bank, when an emotion never experienced before swept down upon me. I said, 'That is what the devout Christian feels, that is how he surrenders his will to the will of God'. I felt an extreme surprise, for my whole imagination was preoccupied with the pagan mythology of ancient Ireland, I was marking in red ink, upon a large map, every sacred mountain. The next morning I awoke near dawn, to hear a voice saying, 'The love of God is infinite for every human soul because every human soul is unique; no other can satisfy the same need in God'.

Lady Gregory and I had heard many tales of changelings, grown men and women as well as children, who, as the people believe, are taken by the faeries, some spirit or inanimate object bewitched into their likeness remaining in their stead, and I constantly asked myself what reality there could be in these tales, often supported by so much testimony. I woke one night to find myself lying upon my back with all my limbs rigid, and to hear a ceremonial measured voice, which did not seem to be mine, speaking through my lips. 'We make an image of him who sleeps', it said 'and it is not he who sleeps, and we call it Emmanuel.' After many years that thought, others often found as strangely being added to it, became the thought of the Mask,[11] which I have used in these memoirs to explain men's characters. A few months ago at Oxford I was asking myself why it should be 'an image of him who sleeps', and took down from the shelf, not knowing what I did, Burkitt's *Early Eastern Christianity,* and opened it at random. I had opened it at a Gnostic Hymn that told of a certain King's son who, being exiled, slept in Egypt—a symbol of the natural state—and how an Angel while he slept brought him a royal mantle; and at the bottom of the page I found a footnote saying that the word mantle did not represent the meaning properly, for that which the Angel gave had the exile's own form and likeness. I did not, however, find in the Gnostic Hymn my other conviction that Egypt and that which the Mask represents are antithetical. That, I think, became clear when a countryman told Lady Gregory and myself that he had heard the crying of new-dropped lambs in November— spring in the world of Faery being November with us.

*   *   *

On the sea-coast at Duras, a few miles from Coole, an old French Count, Florimond de Basterot, lived for certain months in every year. Lady Gregory and I talked over my project of an Irish Theatre,[12] looking out upon the lawn of his house, watching a large flock of ducks that was always gathered for his arrival from Paris, and that would be a very small flock, if indeed it were a flock at all, when he

set out for Rome in the autumn. I told her that I had given up my
project because it was impossible to get the few pounds necessary for
a start in little halls, and she promised to collect or give the money
necessary. That was her first great service to the Irish intellectual
movement. She reminded me the other day that when she first asked
me what she could do to help our movement I suggested nothing;
and, certainly, I no more foresaw her genius than I foresaw that of
John Synge,[13] nor had she herself foreseen it. Our theatre had been
established before she wrote or had any ambition to write,[14] and yet
her little comedies have merriment and beauty, an unusual
combination, and those two volumes where the Irish heroic tales are
arranged and translated in an English so simple and so noble may do
more than other books to deepen Irish imagination. They contain
our ancient literature, are something better than our *Mabinogion*,[15]
are almost our *Morte d'Arthur*. It is more fitting, however, that in a
book of memoirs I should speak of her personal influence, and
especially as no witness is likely to arise better qualified to speak. If
that influence were lacking, Ireland would be greatly impoverished,
so much has been planned out in the library or among the woods at
Coole; for it was there that John Shawe-Taylor[16] found the
independence from class and family that made him summon the
conference between landlord and tenant that brought Land
Purchase,[17] and it was there that Hugh Lane[18] formed those Irish
ambitions that led to his scattering many thousands, and gathering
much ingratitude; and where, but for that conversation at
Florimond de Basterot's, had been the genius of Synge?

I have written these words instead of leaving all to posterity, and
though my friend's ear seems indifferent to praise or blame, that
young men, to whom recent events are often more obscure than
those long past, may learn what debts they owe and to what creditor.

NOTES

Both W.B. Yeats and Lady Gregory confirm that they had met briefly at some literary
function in London in 1895, but the real beginning of the friendship was in August
1896. He and his friend Arthur Symons took the Irish walking-tour that was to have
such momentous consequences, and stayed for a while with Edward Martyn at Tullira
Castle. 'One day Edward Martyn and his mother brought two guests to lunch with me,
Arthur Symons and W.B. Yeats,' Lady Gregory records. 'I had met Yeats before but
had not had any talk with him, and of his writings I had read only his *Celtic Twilight*.'
For their literary collaboration see Elizabeth Coxhead, ' "Collaboration"—Yeats',
Lady Gregory; A Literary Portrait, 2nd ed., revised and enlarged (London: Secker &
Warburg, 1966) pp. 98–107; and Daniel J. Murphy, 'Yeats and Lady Gregory: A
Unique Dramatic Collaboration,' *Modern Drama*, VII, no. 3 (Dec 1964) 322–8.

1. Yeats was a visionary, and he insisted upon surrounding himself with poetic
images. He began a study of the prophetic books of William Blake, the similarly
mystical poet of a century earlier, and this enterprise brought him into contact with
other visionary traditions, such as the Platonic, the Neoplatonic, the Swedenborgian,

and the alchemical. In one of his later prose books, *A Vision* (1925), Yeats gives in terms of frustrating and inspiring spirits one of the clearest and most accurate pictures of poetic inspiration ever drawn.

2. *The Speckled Bird.* Admirers of Yeats will be pleased to learn of the impending publication, by Macmillan of Canada, of this unfinished novel.

3. Gustave Flaubert (1821–80), novelist regarded as the pioneer of the Realist school of French literature.

4. Gustave Flaubert, *La Tentation de Saint Antoine* (1874).

5. Henry More (1614–87), English poet and philosopher of religion whose affinity for the metaphysics of Plato places him among the group of thinkers known as the Cambridge Platonists.

6. This has been solemnly interpreted to mean that Lady Gregory took up folklore-collecting for the benefit of Yeats's health; but of course folklore was her new and chief interest before he appeared personally on the scene.

7. Lady Gregory died on 22 May 1932. Yeats felt her death profoundly, writing the following day: 'I have lost one who has been to me for nearly forty years my strength and my conscience'. He missed Coole as 'the only place where I have ever had unbroken health'. Nor did the sorrow grow less; in 1936 he wrote to Lady Dorothy Wellesley: 'I long for quiet; long ago I used to find it at Coole. It was part of the genius of that house.'

8. Cf. W.B. Yeats, 'The Fiddler of Dooney', *The Wind Among the Reeds* (1899).

9. Cf. W.B. Yeats, 'Under Ben Bulben', *Last Poems* (1936–39).

10. Yeats's first poem on Coole was 'In the Seven Woods'.

11. Yeats's problem was to discover a technique by which the personal could somehow be objectified, be given the appearance of impersonal 'truth' and yet retain the emotive force of privately felt belief. A partial solution was the theory of the Mask which, perhaps compounded from popular psychology on one hand and occult material on the other, was used by Yeats to make public his secret selves.

12. In 1899 the Irish Literary Theatre was born. In 1902 the Irish National Theatre Society, which eventually became the Abbey Theatre in 1904, was founded to continue on a more permanent basis the work begun by the Irish Literary Theatre.

13. Yeats drew Synge, who had planned to devote his life to writing critical articles on French writers, into writing about Irish subjects. He urged him, on one of his visits to Paris, to give up France and to 'go to the Aran Islands and find a life that has never been expressed in Literature'.

14. Lady Gregory entered the theatre at the age of fifty with an unsuspected gift for comedy-writing, which, but for her contact with Yeats and the Irish Dramatic Movement, would presumably never have been realised.

15. A collection of eleven medieval Welsh tales based on mythology, folklore, and heroic legends and recorded from oral stories from the second half of the eleventh century to the close of the thirteenth century.

16. Lady Gregory's nephew.

17. Between 1885 and 1903 a series of land purchase acts (the most important of which was George Wyndham's in 1903) allocated funds to help tenants acquire their own land and offered bonuses to landlords who sold to them. The result was Ireland's transformation from a land of tenant farmers to one of peasant proprietors.

18.. Sir Hugh Percy Lane (1875–1915), Lady Gregory's nephew and art dealer known for his collection of Impressionist paintings. He established a gallery of modern art in Dublin and was appointed Director of the National Gallery of Ireland, Dublin, in 1914. His death in the sinking of the 'Lusitania' stirred a controversy over his collection, the bequest of which was unclear; ultimately it was divided between London and Dublin. See Lady Gregory, *Hugh Lane's life and Achievement, with Some Account of the Dublin Galleries* (London: Murray, 1921).

A Visit to Lady Gregory*

SIGNE TOKSVIG

To get from Dublin to Coole Park, the home of Lady Gregory, one
normally takes a train from Dublin to Athenry, and another from
Athenry to Gort, the village nearest to Coole. But times were not
exactly normal in Ireland when my husband and I visited it last
summer, and when we got to Athenry we were confronted by the
blank fact that for two months or so no trains had been running to
Gort. Why? This was a rhetorical question. We knew very well that
armed policemen must have been trying to travel on that train, and
that the engineer had excused himself for an indefinite period, and
that we had better find a Ford. We found one. It was very rickety and
full of unwieldy first-aid-to-the-injured-auto things, but Gort was
twenty miles away, and hope and beauty had long since left Athenry,
and so we squeezed in and began to bump over stony Connaught.

It is very like stony New England, except for the important fact
that the Pilgrim, after all, had a good-sized field when he had picked
the stones off it and set them up as boundaries, whereas some of
these 'fields' of Connaught were no larger than vegetable beds, it
seemed to me, and yet the stones were piled high around them. Still,
the sun shone a little, and in the pale light of rainy summer this gray-
green landscape had its own wistful charm. Here and there, too, the
madder-red of a Galway petticoat gleamed in a small yellow
cornfield, and girls let their sickles fall to look at us. The country
grew more lonely and more wild. The little fields choked under the
stones. Sheep strayed about, and long-legged, ravenous pigs. No
country estate was visible, and the sun was failing. Then we saw a
long stretch of high gray stone wall and a mass of gloomy trees
behind it. But this was Tillyra, we were told, and we knew it for the
Norman retreat of Edward Martyn, famous in his own right as a
playwright, and also as a large part of George Moore's *Ave atque Vale*.
We were later to visit him, with Lady Gregory, but now we thought
only of Coole Park, and here suddenly it was—gray stone wall,
venerable trees, and a quick, dark-haired woman to open the lodge
gates. For what seemed to me a long while we drove through the

park, still and lovely and darkening in the twilight. After another gate the thick leaves met overhead, and water dripped somewhere in a dim ravine. I had begun to feel that our car was violating Faery, when we drove into a great open meadowy place with haystacks on it, and in the centre, a tall, white, square, unromantic house.

Outside was a little black figure welcoming us. This was Lady Gregory, and as I had never seen her before, I noticed her fresh complexion, bright penetrating brown eyes, white hair black-veiled, slight tendency to stoutness, black mourning clothes and a little black silk apron. She was most cordial, even to me, the unknown marital adjunct of a man whom she knew and liked, and we went into the tall white house.

Now there is one advantage in being young and unimportant and a marital adjunct, and this is that if one is silent, nobody notices. The conversation of the principals goes right on. And meanwhile one is left free to make observations. This inestimable advantage I had most of the time I was at Coole Park, and it thrilled me. Seriously. In an otherwise drab college course on the 'drama,' the great discoveries had been Synge and Yeats and Lady Gregory,—*Riders to the Sea, Cathleen ni Houlihan,* and *The Rising of the Moon.* And here I was free and alone to explore this house, the very hearth where Irish revival had warmed itself.

The drive had been cold, and I sat close to the fire while the principals exchanged comment on absent friends. Lady Gregory wanted to know about John Quinn, and probably she found out, but I looked at the dark, tall, rich room, lit by fluttering candles. Her beautiful warm voice and easy manner went well with this library. The room had been accumulated in no frantic haste. One could imagine its growth from generation to generation until its present opulent age,—worn oriental rugs and curtains, walls of books in old gilt-leather bindings, solid furniture with the sheen of years, and fading red damask coverings. And paintings of frilled men, carvings, statuettes, miniatures, and a real lock of Napoleon's hair under his miniature next to the fireplace.

In the dining-room there was a splendid Zurbaran monk, and that was all I noticed until, candle in hand, Lady Gregory led me up the wide stairs to my room. The walls above the stairs were covered with sketches by Augustus John and Jack Yeats, and rows of eminent, engraved Englishmen who had been members of a famous breakfast club to which Sir William Gregory had belonged. They looked almost incredibly mild, dignified, and benevolent. Altogether different was an aggressive little sketch of Lady Gregory by Augustus John, far from flattering, but one which I could see represented something in her character—an angular fighting mood, which probably has carried her through many a storm at the Abbey Theatre. Not that I know that there ever have been any storms at the Abbey; this is only a supposition of mine, drawn from long observation of other small groups working together for the betterment, artistic or political, of their community.

Lady Gregory left me in my room with the casual remark that the Shaws (G. Bernard) always had this room, and that he might have been there at that very moment if he hadn't had to go to Parknasilla in Kerry. I think it was Parknasilla, but I felt with a reverential thirll that at least an epigram of his might still be lurking in the black shadows made blacker by my trembling candle. It was a cavernous room. I barely saw tapestried chairs and books and a huge white-frilled canopied bed. There were roses on a white dressing table. I went to open a window. It opened on the thickest, darkest, chilliest, quietest night that ever was since the creation of night. The darkness stole into the room and buried my candle, and the silence made my thoughts seem loud. I knew then why poets come to Coole.

The quietude of Coole I shall always remember. During the week I was there it seemed to me ludicrous to believe that the crossing of Broadway and Sixth Avenue was in the same world. Through the big house the maids moved almost unseen and always unheard. With one exception. One night after dinner we were sitting in the library, and, unbelievable as it seemed, there were human voices coming from the dining-room. Lady Gregory got up, opened the door softly, and looked in. She said nothing, only looked for an instant, but that conversation stopped as if cut off with a knife. This was the only time we saw our hostess as a grande dame. Otherwise she was as simple and friendly with her servants as she was with the farmers roundabout, with her friends and with her guests. But she couldn't tolerate the breaking of the seal of silence. For one who wasn't doing creative work, Coole was almost uncomfortably quiet. I came near to a feeling of relief one morning when I heard from Lady Gregory's work-room a certain staccato sound that I knew well, and learned that she wrote her plays on a typewriter, and not, as I in my innocence had supposed, with a swan's quill.

That afternoon I found the garden. The rare glow of sunshine lay on the high gray walls, hung with yellow drooping roses and reddening vines and waxy white flowers. A broad shadowed walk ran the length of the wall. There was an enchanting vista of it from the garden gate. I went slowly along, crushing rosemary between my fingers, and wondering at the dark groups of stately Irish yews. At the end of the garden I found a gate in the wall, a big, old, rusty and green gate through which I peered at a wet wilderness of trees and mossy stones. One path plunged into it, but I couldn't tease the gate open. So I turned, and behind me, under a huge tree, I found a little graveyard. At least I found three pathetic small headstones—one for

'Poor Little Prinnie,' dead in 1800, another for 'Trim,' and another for 'Gyp'. I sentimentalized a bit. Up the garden, on the other side I discovered a sort of shrine of dark bending boughs and clustering ivy screening a Roman bust—Virgil, I thought, or Quintus Horatius Flaccus, set there by eighteenth century admiration. A little further on I met Lady Gregory, red-cheeked, brown-eyed, black-robed, with a nice housewifely basket on her arm. She gave me a bunch of grapes. Encouraged by this into asking questions, I said, 'Would you mind telling me the history of that bust over there?' 'Not at all,' she answered, 'that's a bust of Maecenas. We used to have him in the little bathroom downstairs, and got very tired of him there, and so we put him outside,' Well, there wasn't much romance here, and I tried the little graveyard. 'Oh, that's where my husband's mother used to bury her pug-dogs. She was very fond of pug-dogs,' I dropped the attempt to discover Romance for myself.

Lady Gregory was a better guide. She took me first to her 'autograph tree,' a big copper-beech, not very coppery, but blessed beyond all other trees in a trunk full of monograms that cover the whole Irish literary revival. I cannot remember them all. There was 'G.B.S.' for George Bernard Shaw,—the boldest letters of them all,—and a modest 'J.M.S.' for Synge, a 'W.B.Y.' for Yeats, a 'J.B.' and a small donkey for his brother Jack, a 'D.H.' for Douglas Hyde, and 'A.E.' for George Russell, a new white 'L.R.' for Lennox Robinson, an 'A.J.' for Augustus John, and others and others and others.

Then we went to the big gate at the end of the garden, and in it there was a little door that I hadn't seen before, and near the door hung a large key, and the key opened the door. We were in the Seven Woods of Coole.

It had rained all summer, and masses of foliage clung together, dripping, overgrown. Black wet branches, patched with livid fungi, twisted before us, and mosses and ferns ran in thick waves over the path, over stones, over every fallen tree. It was an orgy of greens and rotting browns. And the stillness was deeper than night. I began to glance covertly at Lady Gregory, and tried to think of Yeats's—

> I know of the leafy paths that the witches take,
> Who come with their crowns of pearl and their spindles of wool,
> And their secret smile, out of the depths of the lake. ...[1]

She had said she was going to take me down to the lake, and she was talking about wool. But it was wool in the form of twenty-four fleeces. They and some carriage blankets had been stolen from a loft not long ago. 'And did you go to the police?' I inquired idly, pricking up my ears quickly enough when she said, 'Oh no, I went to the Sinn Fein Volunteers, and in a week they had caught the thief and restored the things. Now I have asked them to find out who took a wire fence

I'd recently set up.' I wanted to ask many more questions about
Republican Ireland, but I knew she preferred not to talk 'politics.'

Instead, she talked forestry. Lady Gregory cares for the seven
woods in a very practical way, and she showed me groves of young
trees and saplings she had had planted. 'Nearly all my book royalties
grow into trees,' she said. I liked the commonsense streak in her.
Gradually I was beginning to find that she kept herself in no aesthetic
citadel, that the hospitality of her mind was as generous as her house.
I began to see that a poet could also be a wise and straightforward
human being; something which before had only seemed true of A.E.
She talked of America, without a taint of even benevolent
condescension, and with a surprising affection. 'I had to go over
there just before Christmas, and I hated to spend the holidays away
from my family on the rough, cold, gray Atlantic, and in a new
country; and then the people over there amazed me by taking me
into their homes, and being so kind to me that I shall never forget it.'

It began to be a long walk through the wet strange woods, and I
saw no lake, but this I forgot when she mentioned Yeats, and told me
how he had come there year after year, bringing the very people who
needed Coole. That, naturally, she didn't say, still it is apparent what
wild, simple, lovely Connaught has done for the work of Jack Yeats,
for instance, who was painting conventional sweet pictures of
Devonshire before his brother brought him to Coole. She told me—
and this somehow made the woods enchanted—that Synge had liked
to run through them and by the lake for hours and hours.

Very soon after, we came to the lake.

It is long and rather narrow, and the woods recede a little from it,
leaving a green strand with a path lightly marked on moss and
grasses. Far out, sailing around dark islets, I saw the wild swans of
Coole, shy guests of every autumn. On another walk when I was
alone and could indulge myself I picked up two of their white curling
feathers, making the mean excuse to myself of needing souvenirs. I
don't know where they are now, but I remember finding them at the
sombre edge of the woods, and peering in and being afraid to go
further, because I had the property of the swans in my pocket and the
green stillness was faintly threatening. If I must confess it, I ran all
the way home, with a sudden black squall chasing at my heels in
what seemed to me a very personal manner. Luckily, I didn't have to
run through the woods, since on the first walk Lady Gregory took me
home by a short cut through the fields. Let those who want to,
laugh,—after an experience I had on a fairy island in Kerry I make
apologies to no one.

The next day I was alone in the high silent library with my hostess.
Until then she had treated me with exquisite courtesy and
consideration, but strictly as a member of the general category

'guest.' Now, in her quick way, she left her desk and sat down next me. As her bright brown eyes fixed mine I felt myself changing from a guest to an individual. 'Tell me what you have done, and what you are going to do,' she said, and the tone of her voice completed the change in me. It was warm and kind, and uncomfortably full of concentration on me—not on me as the inoffensive marital adjunct of a visiting friend, but me as a body expected to answer for my real self. I don't mean by this that her tone held me up and demanded the immediate unfolding of my soul, as I was once held up by a wealthy suburban woman who asked me loudly in front of a number of people, 'Now come, what's your specialty? Tell me all about yourself and what your specialty is.' Both times I felt uneasy at being dragged from a decent obscurity, but the causes were entirely different. Before the achievements of Lady Gregory one had a right to shrink from uncovering the disordered perfunctoriness of one's own past and future. And then she showed me that dispelling uneasiness was another of her achievements. I realized how it is that she has become a recorder of the withdrawn songs and legends of the 'thatched houses,' and how it is that she learned their speech, not only Gaelic but their cadenced, colored English, 'the Gaelic construction, the Elizabethan phrases,' the quick turn and fresh invention. I felt—as farmers, stone-cutters, workhouse wards, beggars must have felt— that here was a woman without mockery, a human being without mockery, a human being in whom there was the safety of kindness, and a keen simplicity of interest that warranted understanding. Those who have read her own creative works and compilations of Irish poetry, history and legend, and who know the Irish peasant, will know how faithfully and beautifully she has preserved this amazingly imaginative language. Synge knew it, and learned from her 'the dialect he had been trying to master.' Yeats knew it, and she collaborated with him in the writing of most of his plays, especially *Cathleen ni Houlihan.*

I can't help quoting from her life of Raftery, a Connaught poet, whose songs she patiently gathered from the memories of the countryside. It is from Raftery's Lament for Thomas O'Daly, a fiddler and piper: 'The swans on the water are nine times blacker than a blackberry since the man died from us that had pleasantness on the top of his fingers. His two gray eyes were like the dew of the morning that lies on the grass. And since he was laid in the grave, the cold is getting the upper hand.' Lady Gregory says about this poem, 'I have been helped to put it into English by a young working farmer, sitting by a turf fire one evening, when his day in the fields was over.'

Even in my short stay in the barony of Kiltartan, I heard phrases of delight, fragments of wit and rhythm, that made me wish for a good memory more than anything else has ever done. This was John, Lady

Gregory's coachman, and one thing he said I shall never forget. We were driving back from Gort through the leafy twilight of the park, and I tried very cautiously to see how John felt about the fairies. He pooh-poohed them eagerly, almost too eagerly. 'Why, Miss, there's no one would go near this place after dark, but many a night I've stayed up with a sick cow and never seen anything in it worse than myself.' Then he grew thoughtful, and pointed with his whip to a path that ran up a little hill. 'Do you see the rabbits now, and they running up that hill?' I did. 'Well,' continued John, 'there last week, I set a trap for them, and never one of them came near the hill. Then I took it away. And that same night they all came trooping back, till you wouldn't know was it right rabbits were in it!' He paused and laughed a little nervously. Then he said—and this is my prize souvenir: 'Would you be knowing a gentleman, I wonder, who used to come here every year to stay with her ladyship? His name was Mr. Yeats. He was always running around in the woods a'snipin' for the fairies.'

Both for that exquisite picture and for many others I am grateful to gentle John Devaney.

The night before we left, I think it was, Lady Gregory read to us from her life of Sir Hugh Lane. I, being ignorant of most English and Irish affairs, really knew nothing about Sir Hugh Lane except that he was a great collector of old masters, and an art dealer, and that he was drowned on the *Lusitania*. I didn't know that he was Lady Gregory's nephew. This relationship disquieted me a little, because In Memoriams, even of strangers, are seldom real. So when she began to read from the proofs my attention was merely polite. This indifference lasted less than a minute. In the first place, Lady Gregory reads so beautifully that one can't help listening to her; in the second place (which really ought to be the first) the *Life of Sir Hugh Lane* is an appealing, adventurous, honest book. I doubt if anything Lady Gregory has ever written is as simple and beautiful as the first chapters describing her sister, Adelaide Persse, her unhappy marriage to Mr Lane, and the brave youth of the son Hugh. And the story of his self-denials and his successes is almost uncannily interesting. It is an Aladdin romance with a tragic ending.

From that evening we learned clearly that the passion of Lady Gregory is to help preserve and develop the arts of Ireland. What she has done in the literary field is well known; it is not so well known that since her nephew's death she has been trying to carry on his work. He bent his life toward giving Dublin a great museum of art, so that the students of art might have worthy models. On an accidental technicality in his will, London acquired half the masterpieces that were meant for Dublin. Lady Gregory has been working ever since trying to get them back. She told us of her hopes for the Municipal Gallery in Dublin, with its portraits of famous Irishmen of the new generation, and where she also wants portraits of Irishmen who have become famous elsewhere. 'Can't you get some American to donate a painting of Peter Dunne?' she asked. And then we talked about the Abbey theatre, and about the all too enchanting idea of having a real Abbey theatre in New York to which the Dublin players could 'graduate,' so to speak.

The following day Lady Gregory drove us to Galway, the next stage in our journey. That drive is vivid in my mind. As we went through Gort, she showed us the workhouse, a gray and ivied building, where she had sat many an evening by the turf-fire, quietly listening to such good purpose as *The Workhouse Wards* and many a resurrected poem and legend prove. Soon we left the green fields around Gort and came into a country that was like a world petrified. If the stretch between Athenry and Gort was stony, that between Gort and Burren was stone itself. It was the waste dominion of stone. Hills of it slept in the distance, the fields were great gray sheets of it, and only where it broke into boulders and pebbles a few sheep nibbled faint grass-straws. At long intervals a thatched hut clung to the smooth rock, but for miles we were alone with the hard grayness. And then a miracle happened. A cloudy sunlight shone and all the stone turned to silver. Yet 'silver' is too simple a word to use about the soft luminous white of the naked hills that rose before us in long unbroken lines against a sky where blue melted into green above them. That radiance was unearthly, and, partly to come back to earth, I made the sage remark that certainly no life had ever existed on those barren hills, without so much as a suspicion of moss on them. Lady Gregory smiled. 'Indeed it has,' she said. 'Here was a favourite resort of the holy hermits; traces of them have been found on top of the hills.'

'What did they have to eat?' I asked brutally, and she answered, 'I know what one of them had once,' and I begged for the story. The story was that one of the holy men who lived by himself up there in sacred meditation came of very good family. In fact, his brother was a king, King Guaire of Connaught. The saint's name was Marbhan. Now one day the king was sitting down to a particularly good dinner—it was really more in the nature of a banquet, and, being a very kind man as well as a king, he said to his courtiers, 'Isn't it the shame of the world that here we sit with a fine dinner before us, and there is my poor brother up in the Burren hills with nothing but watercress and maybe a handful of nuts?' No sooner had he said this than, presto, unseen hands removed the dinner, and in a twinkling had it before the saint, who, it is to be hoped, ate it. Imprints of angelic footsteps are still to be seen on the Burren hills.

'You never heard of King Guaire?' Lady Gregory asked. I shook my head. 'Why, he was so generous,' she said, 'that his right arm grew longer than his left, because he stretched it out so often to give alms to the poor. And he was so kind that once when his royal cloak had caught on a bush he couldn't bear to take it away from the bush but left it right there. And he was rewarded for that. He had a great many poets at his court, and the wives of the poets were full of many whims, and sometimes it wasn't easy to fulfil the laws of hospitality. In the middle of winter one poet's wife insisted that she must have some blackberries. The good king sent messengers far and wide, but there were no blackberries to be had. He sent them out again, and this time one of them came back with a basketful. *Where* had he found them? Ah, on a bush covered with the king's own royal cloak under which they had ripened nicely.' And then, as Lady Gregory says in *Saints and Wonders,* where I later found the same story, 'then there was no reproach on the King's house.'

Soon we were over the hills in Burren, the Atlantic was wide before us, and we rested a while in the pleasant little sea lodge that belongs to Coole Park. Then we drove on through Kinvara and Oranmore to Galway. Often on the road, English military lorries full of soldiers with rifles at the ready made our little car skip for its and our lives, and I saw Lady Gregory's face grow stern. Nobody spoke. In Galway we said good-bye to her.

That week at Coole made many impressions on me, but none deeper than one night when, candle in hand, Lady Gregory was saying good night to me and added: 'Now I'm going to say my prayer for the Lord Mayor of Cork. I've said it every evening since he has been on hunger strike. It is the one in the prayer book for a sick person "when there appeareth small hope of recovery." ' She said this with an expression and a warmth which left me feeling that here was a woman who loved Ireland of the present as well as Ireland of the past. She, also, will have helped make possible the Ireland of the future.

NOTES

Signe Toksvig (Mrs Francis Hackett) is the author of *The Last Devil* (London, 1927) *The Life of Hans Christian Andersen* (London, 1933), *Eve's Doctor* (London, 1937), *Port of Refuge* (London, 1938), *Life Boat, A Novel* (London, 1941), and *Emanuel Swedenborg, Scientist and Mystic* (London, 1949).

1. W.B. Yeats, 'The Withering of the Boughs', *In the Seven Woods* (1904).

Lady Gregory at Rehearsals*

MAIRE NIC SHIUBHLAIGH

Lady Gregory, now an established member of the committee,[1] paid Camden Street[2] occasional visits. These usually took place with the approach of new plays when she forsook the quiet of Coole House, her home at Gort, County Galway, and took rooms in a Dublin Hotel, entertaining lavishly during her stay. As the work of new dramatists wishing to avail of the society[3] passed from Fay's hands through a reading committee to her, before we saw it, she always insisted on reading over selected pieces to us in her hotel drawing-room. Her odd lisping voice had a peculiar effect on speeches, especially those of the poetic sort, and, later, the strange lilting lines of J.M. Synge, which suffered much through her pronunciation. I think she rather fancied herself as an actress. Years later, when circumstances delayed my arrival at the Abbey for an appearance as Kathleen Ni Houlihan,[4] she horrified Yeats and the company by calmly announcing that she would play the part herself. Her interpretation was hardly a flattering one, not only because of her extraordinary sing-song delivery of the beautiful lines. Her appearance, at times oddly reminiscent of an elderly Queen Victoria, can hardly have been in keeping with the character[5] Yeats had in mind when he wrote the play. But her arrival in such fashion as an Abbey Theatre actress, received, to her delight and Yeats' dismay, widespread publicity, and she often spoke of the occasion afterwards, referring proudly and a trifle pathetically to her appearance in the play as the realisation of a life-long ambition.

But she was a pleasant if at times rather condescending person, who treated us all rather as children in need of special advice. A member of a well-known Galway family, the Persses, and the widow of a former British Colonial official, Sir William Gregory, of the neighbouring house of Coole, she was drawn almost by chance into the dramatic movement. She has written somewhere of meeting Yeats in London in 1898, and being struck by his theories of playwriting and his hope to one day found a theatre for the

*The Splendid Years: Recollections of Maire Nic Shiubhlaigh, As Told to Edward Kenny (Dublin: James Duffy, 1955) pp. 29–32.

production of experimental plays. It was after this, her interest in the drama aroused, that she joined in launching the Literary Theatre. When this failed, she turned, like Yeats, to the most promising of its successors and came to us in 1902, a small, not very striking woman in middle age, full of a great enthusiasm for our work and a conviction that the Irish National Theatre Society should succeed where the Literary Theatre had failed. In these and later years she frequently had her own way as far as the affairs of the society were concerned, for although she was not altogether overbearing, she was tenacious, which is much the same thing. I have many memories of her during these years; presiding maternally at one of those lavish suppers she loved to hold in the theatre on first nights; or, in different circumstances, drawing up her short rather bulky figure, squaring her shoulders and smiling rather grimly in a thin-lipped manner in face of opposition. Or again in later years, bustling with her strange, short-stepped walk through the Abbey, meeting distinguished visitors in the vestibule before the curtain rose on new plays, smiling her rather fixed social smile, or talking rapidly in her odd flat-toned way. Her interest in the theatre was profound, and with the years it quickened. When, in 1910, she assumed part control of the Abbey, the theatre became for her a life interest—as she wrote herself, one of her 'enthusiasms'. She was the Abbey's self-appointed champion, and doubtless but for her perseverance, the theatre might have closed its doors during the lean years through which it passed after its establishment as an independent concern, its control vested in a directorate. With Yeats, she fought all its battles and surmounted all its difficulties.

She was a most hospitable hostess. During these early years, her arrival in Dublin for a new play was usually accompanied by an invitation to the Nassau Hotel, where in her austerely-furnished suite, she would entertain a few of us elegantly with tea and French cakes while she discussed forthcoming productions. Occasionally, too, she would have quantities of confectionery sent down to Camden Street, coming in herself later in the evening and, rather like an understanding aunt, sitting beside the stove while we brewed tea and ate. It was in Camden Street during a rehearsal of her play *Twenty-five*[6] that she instituted what was later to become one of the most popular features of Abbey Theatre first nights—the 'Gort Barm-brack suppers'. The Gort Barm-brack was a huge cartwheel of a fruit-cake, filled with the richest ingredients, made specially by her own bakers at Gort for the casts of any of her new plays. It was a huge affair of several pounds weight and usually took two to carry it. It must have been two feet in circumference, and fully eight inches in depth. Wrapped around with silver paper, bits of candied peel and glacé cherries sticking out all over its shiny surface, it held a place of honour on a table near the stove. I will always connect barm-brack with rehearsals and the smell of grease-paint. Abbey openings years later would never have been considered complete if there was not one—and it had to be a genuine Gort one—on the table in the green-room, with a serrated knife beside it for anyone who wanted a piece. Many times have I gulped the last crumb of a slice down before stepping on to the Abbey stage, and many times has my reluctance to part with any of it, even after my cue had come and gone, made me temporarily inarticulate before the footlights.

NOTES

One of the player-founders of the Irish National Theatre, Maire Nic Shiubhlaigh witnessed the Abbey Theatre's early trials and triumphs. She was a moving spirit in the interesting Theatre of Ireland and Edward Martyn's Irish Theatre, before she played her most important role in a Republican garrison during Easter Week in 1916.

1. The Irish National Theatre Society was to be a purely cooperative one with a committee which would defer to the desires of the society as a whole, each member—whether actor or committee-man—to have an interest in the affairs of the group, the choice of plays, etc.

2. The headquarters of the Irish National Theatre Society was a modest hall at 34 Camden Street, Dublin.

3. The Irish National Theatre Society.

4. *Cathleen Ni Houlihan,* by W.B. Yeats, opened at St Teresa's Hall, Clarendon Street, Dublin, on 22 April 1902, with Maud Gonne as Cathleen and Maire Nic Shiubhlaigh as Delia Cahel. In March 1919, a revival of the play was due, and Maire Nic Shiubhlaigh, the Cathleen, suddenly found that she could not appear for the first three nights. Rather than postpone the play, Lady Gregory volunteered to act the part herself; 'after all, what is wanted but a hag and a voice?'

5. Maud Gonne, with whom Yeats was in love.

6. *Twenty-five* was first presented at the Molesworth Hall, Dublin on 14 March 1903. Maire Nic Shiubhlaigh played the part of Kate Ford.

*Kincora**

WILLIAM G. FAY

In March we broke entirely new ground with a three-act play[1] by Lady Gregory, which was particularly welcome because it dealt with a popular subject in historical legend—the life of Brian Boru,[2] or 'Brian of all the talents.' You see that made it a safe proposition, and it had the further advantage of being long enough to fill the whole

*Extracted from *The Fays of the Abbey Theatre* (London: Rich & Cowan, 1935) pp. 170–2.

evening without a forepiece. Special scenery and costumes were
designed by Lady Gregory's son Robert and painted and made in the
theatre. In the case of the scenery it was Robert Gregory's first
experience of having to enlarge a finished design to something many
times the size of the original. But he was eager to learn and worked
hard with me in the paint room. When the last scene, 'The Wood of
Clontarf,' was finished it provided a new sensation for Dublin in
those days; for, instead of the orthodox wood scene showing dozens
of trees with every leaf stippled on to them, it was just a pattern of
boles of trees with a leaf design applied in one colour, the whole
giving a rhythmic effect of greens and greys.

On the first night the theatre was completely filled for the first time
since our opening night, and the play met with unqualified approval.
The Press for once was most friendly. Even *The United Irishman* agreed
that the play was worth producing. Lady Gregory certainly showed
great skill in combining historical accuracy with dramatic quality, by
no means always an easy matter. The play was further notable for
being one of the earliest attempts to get rid of the 'tushery' which has
always been the bane of period drama. By the time she wrote
Devorgilla[3] she had perfected her method so that there is not a trace of
incongruity in the modern diction of her characters. Recently in
Tobias and the Angel Mr. James Bridie[4] has brilliantly shown how the
same method can be applied to a Biblical subject.

As soon as the production and the plaudits were over, Robert
Gregory returned to London to resume his work at the Salde School.
A few weeks later Lady Gregory casually mentioned to me that she
had just had a letter from her son to say that he had been in bed with
a cold but was now better and at work again. However, as is the
nature of anxious mothers, she seemed to worry a bit, and presently
she said, 'You won't want me here for a day or two, so I think I'll run
over to London to see how he is myself. I should feel easier. Don't tell
anyone where I have gone or they will be making a fuss. I will be
back by Friday.' And so she went forthwith. Next morning, when I
came down town, the first person I met greeted me with 'Have you
heard the news about Robert Gregory?' I said no. 'Oh, he has been
taken very ill and rushed off to hospital.' I said I hoped it was nothing
serious, and passed on, only to encounter another who was bursting
with news. 'Have you heard about Robert Gregory?' he said. 'He is so
ill his mother has been wired for and she has rushed off by the night
boat for London.' Half an hour later I was informed by somebody
else that Robert had been run down by a bus, then that he had been
run over by a taxi, presently that one of his legs would have to be
amputated below the knee, and finally that both his legs were so
mangled that he would have to go about on crutches for the rest of
his life. By the time Lady Gregory got back to Dublin there wasn't

much left of Robert. The truth, of course, was that, as he had said, he had only had a slight cold and she might have saved herself her trouble. When I told her what a fine story Dublin had made of it all she laughed heartily and replied, 'And people said that *Spreading the News*⁵ was an improbable play!'

NOTES

William George (1872–1947) and Frank J. (1870–1931) Fay were Irish actors who were important in the early history of the Abbey Theatre. They began their careers at the Dublin Dramatic School, run by Mrs Lacy, wife of a touring manager. In 1898 they formed the Armonde Dramatic Society. When the Irish National Theatre Society was founded in 1902 it included the two actors. Stephen Gwynn, in *Irish Literature and Drama,* says: 'The style of acting identified with the Abbey Theatre is due to the genius of the Fays—and with W.G. Fay especially.' William Fay left the Abbey and went to America in 1908.

1. *Kincora* was first produced at the Abbey Theatre on 25 March 1905.
2. Semi-mythical chief and High King of Ireland, killed at the battle of Clontarf (1014).
3. The first night of *Devorgilla* was at the Abbey Theatre on 31 October 1907.
4. James Bridie (1888–1951), Scottish dramatist and medical practitioner, whose visits to the Abbey players and other itinerant theatrical attractions had aroused his latent interest in the theatre.
5. The first performance of *Spreading the News* was at the Abbey Theatre on 27 December 1904.

'We Must Teach Them'*

JOSEPH HOLLOWAY

Thursday, November 29 [1906]. A violent storm accompanied by rain swept over the city during the evening and night, preventing many from leaving their homes, I have no doubt. Be it from that or other causes, I found but a handful at the Abbey, and Henderson¹ quite disconsolate in the vestibule. Yeats, having so much space to wander about it, kept continually on the move. Lady Gregory also looked gloomy, and after *Deirdre*² asked me, 'What has become of the audience?' I could only say that, 'Perhaps they don't like verse plays.' And she said, 'Then we must teach them to like them!'

I then spoke of the regard people had for AE's *Deirdre,* and she

*Extracted from *Joseph Holloway's Abbey Theatre: A Selection from His Unpublished Journal 'Impressions of a Dublin Playgoer',* ed. Robert Hogan and Michael J. O'Neill (Carbondale and Edwardsville: Southern Illinois University Press; London and Amsterdam: Feffer & Simons, 1967) pp. 76–7.

wondered if they were so fond of it that the Theatre of Ireland[3] people did not play it; there was nothing to prevent them doing so. I showed her the post card I had received re the first performance of the Theatre of Ireland at the Molesworth Hall next week, and she said she was sorry they were not producing anything new, as everything new in the dramatic way helped the movement along ....

I saw Yeats's *Deirdre* played for the second time to-night and must confess that I thought it tame and lifeless. ... Sensuality is over the entire play, and nightly-decreasing audiences testify to the lack of interest taken in such-like work. Miss Darragh's 'Deirdre' does not improve on acquaintance; it lacks sincerity and charm.

NOTES

In 1904 Miss A.E. Horniman, a benevolent Englishwoman, allowed the Irish National Theatre Society an annual subsidy and undertook at her own expense the renovation of the old theatre of the Mechanics' Institute in Abbey Street, Dublin and lent it rent-free for six years to the Society. The entire restoration and decoration of the 'Abbey Theatre' was the work of Irish hands. The architect was Joseph Holloway, C.E., of Dublin. Holloway was a steady supporter of the company and for many years he kept a diary in which he recorded not only his reactions to the plays but also his descriptions of Dublin's leading figures. 'Impressions of a Dublin Playgoer', which runs to some 25 million words jotted down hastily on more than 100,000 pages, is in the National Library of Ireland and for years has been consulted by scholars from all over the world.

1. W.A. Henderson, Manager of the Irish National Theatre Society. Like Joseph Holloway, Henderson kept a diary. See also W.A. Henderson, 'The Irish Theatre Movement', *Sunday Independent* (Dublin) XVII, no. 38 (17 Sep 1922).

2. *Deirdre,* by W.B Yeats, had its première at the Abbey Theatre on 24 November 1906. In *Our Irish Theatre,* Lady Gregory says: 'I worked as well at the plot and the construction of some of the poetic plays, especially *The King's Threshold* and *Deirdre.*'

3. The Theatre of Ireland was a new offshoot of the prolific dramatic tree of the Irish literary movement. 'Personally,' says Holloway in his Diaries, 'I should like to see the branches lopped off, and the sap restored to the parent tree.'

What Lady Gregory Said*

Lady Gregory, in a conversation with a *Freeman's Journal* reporter, stated—We have already declared publicly this winter that, in the opinion of those conducting this theatre, it is the fiddler who chooses the tune. The public are quite at liberty to stay away, but if they come in they must take what is provided for them. 'The Playboy,' she

Evening Telegraph (Dublin) (29 Jan 1907) p. 2.

added, will be produced at the Abbey Theatre every night during the week, as originally arranged.

NOTES

W.B. Yeats drew Synge, who had planned to devote his life to writing critical articles on French writers, into writing about Irish subjects. He urged him, on one of his visits to Paris, to give up France and 'to go to the Aran Islands and find a life that has never been expressed in literature'. In 'The Municipal Gallery Revisited' he says:

> John Synge, I and Augusta Gregory, thought
> All that we did, all that we said or sang
> Must come from contact with the soil

Synge reached the greatest height of comedy in *The Playboy of the Western World,* the fullest and most elaborate of all his works. In this play Christy Mahon, a shy youth, becomes a hero when he reveals that he has slain, as he thinks, his domineering father. He triumphs in the local sports and wins the spirited Pegeen Mike away from her terrified fiancé. However, when Christy's father, Old Mahon, arrives, and Christy tries to kill him again, he loses his glamour as a hero, even with Pegeen. When the play opened on Saturday night, 26 January 1907, there were riots at the Abbey Theatre. The objections against the play were made on religious, moral and patriotic grounds. On religious grounds, the audience objected that the play's references to God, the Catholic Church, and the sacrament of marriage were blasphemous and profane. On moral grounds, the play's attitude to parricide was found to be equivocal and morally indefensible. The third line of attack was that the play was unpatriotic and likely to reflect discredit on Ireland. These objections were raised either by perfectly sincere Nationalists or by political coteries. See James Kilroy, *The 'Playboy' Riots* (Dublin: Dolmen Press, 1971); and W.B. Yeats's description of the events in *The Arrow* (Dublin) I, no. 3 (23 Feb 1907).

A Weeding-Out of Words*

There was comparative calm in the Abbey Theatre last night when 'The Playboy of the Western World' was again produced. The audience was smaller than on any night since the production of the play, which has been received with such a storm of disapproval. The fact that there was little disorder enabled those present to form a more correct impression of the character of the play than could hitherto be gained.

A few minutes before eight o'clock the pit and balcony were fairly well filled, but there were only a couple of dozen in the stalls. The 'pitites' were manifestly antagonistic to the play. Before the curtain

*Extracted from '*The Playboy* Has a Quieter Time at the Abbey,' *Evening Herald* (Dublin) (1 Feb 1907) p. 5.

rose on 'Riders of the Sea' [*sic*] they sang 'The Man of the West' with much vigour, and when Mr W.B. Yeats made his appearance he was received with hisses and boohs. The singing of 'A Nation Once Again' was started, and continued until the curtain-raiser was produced. As was the case on the nights previous, 'Riders of the Sea' was well-received.

RECEIVED WITH A HOWL

There was an interval of some 15 minutes before 'The Playboy' was produced. In the meantime the crowd in the stalls was reinforced by a number of young men who, judging from their subsequent applause, were approvers of the play. The vast majority of the audience was, however, decidedly hostile. The first act had scarcely opened when there was a storm of boohing and hissing, which drowned the voices of those on the stage for several minutes. The police who, to the number of 30 or more, were lined up on either side of the pit, displayed much activity, but, apparently, they did not discover anybody whose conduct called for removal, and so the 'chucking out' process was not resorted to. There was a howl when the 'Playboy,' Christopher Mahon, appeared, and, after preliminary conversation with 'Pegeen Mike' and her father announced that he was a parricide. The display of hostility was intensified when 'Pegeen,' on the strength of his declaration, showed towards him the most effusive affection. There was some applause, but it was drowned in the expressions of disapproval.

Shortly after the opening of Act II, Mr Synge, the author, walked out through the stage door and took a seat in the stalls. He was greeted with hisses and some applause. It is in this act Christopher Mahon is greeted with 'a thousand welcomes' because he is the man who killed his father, and when the greeting was extended it was followed by loud boohing.

WAS IT INFLUENZA?

At this point a new form of interruption was invented. Everybody in the pit seemed to be attacked by a violent fit of coughing and sneezing, which lasted a couple of minutes. The supposed parricide was meantine on the stage conversing with 'Pegeen Mike,' but few heard what he said, and when the coughing and sneezing ceased there were cries of 'Lynchehaun!' 'Rotten,' and 'Go in.' The disorder did not continue, however, and the curtain went down on Act II without any exciting incident taking place.

As soon as the lights were turned on for the interval a young man in the body of the pit began to sing, in stentorian tones, 'The Man of the West,' and the chorus was taken up by many voices. The audience was then treated to 'The West's Asleep,' and so the time went on until Act III began.

Again there was an outburst of hissing, but this time it was of a mild character, and, a few minutes later, a number of young men walked ostentatiously out from the pit shouting as they went—'Rotten.' It seemed as if there was about to be a disturbance, and the police were again active, while voices from the stalls called out 'No Suppression.'

A CALMER ENDING

In a brief space quiet was again restored, to be broken by a momentary altercation between two gentlemen who occupied seats at the back of the stalls. They separated after exchanging 'courtesies,' and the remainder of the proceedings may be described as tame. It is true that there was much booing when the curtain dropped, but there was also no inconsiderable applause, and the angry passions which were manifested at the conclusion of the previous nights' performances were altogether absent. The theatre was empty in the space of a few minutes without any efforts on the part of the police.

Outside there was a large force of police, while at the junction of Abbey Street and O'Connell Street another body of men was posted. The crowds which had collected were moved on, and at 11 o'clock the utmost order prevailed.

Early in the night two young men who are alleged to have been creating a disturbance in the theatre were arrested, and taken to Store Street Station. They were subsequently released on bail, and will be charged in the Police Court this morning.

A WEEDING-OUT OF WORDS

Lady Gregory, seen at the conclusion of the performance, expressed her pleasure at the hearing accorded to the play. 'If Friday and Saturday nights' performances are equally satisfactory, "The Playboy" season will end this week; if not, it will be continued until the management consider that everyone wishing to hear it has had a fair opportunity of having his wish fulfilled.'

Has not the play been considerably pruned, and have not some of the expressions to which the greatest objection was made been deleted?

'Very little change has been made,' said Lady Gregory, 'It is true that a few adjectives have been taken out, as have been most of the invocations of the Holy Name, but curiously enough the words and phrases to which most objection has been raised have not been interfered with.'

Lady Gregory added that a suggestion had been made that if the prices of admission were raised the disorder would have ceased at once. But they had too much confidence in the good sense of the general public to adopt that course, and she considered that the comparative tranquillity that night justified their confidence.

She continued that she had been offered considerable support from the 'classes'—what some people, she said, would call the 'Castle dinner' set—if such plays as 'Kathleen ni Houlihan' were not staged. But she had declined. Another section would object to some other play, and so on until the management would be reduced to musical comedy without the comedy—simply the music.

An Exciting Experience*

WALTER STARKIE

The most exciting theatrical experience of my youth took place in my thirteenth year when J.M. Synge's play *The Playboy of the Western World* was produced for the first time at the Abbey Theatre in January 1907. It was my first visit to the Abbey Theatre, and Paddy Tobin, whom at school we all considered an expert in theatrical matters as he had acted with his three cousins, the Wogan Brown girls (all of them excellent actresses, and one of them, Dorothy, so vivacious that she appealed to Bernard Shaw as the ideal embodiment of Dolly in *You Never Can Tell*), promised to bring me round to the Green Room to introduce me to Lady Gregory.

'Tonight,' he said, when I met him at Nelson's Pillar, 'my father says there will be the hell of a row as the newspapers have been publishing attacks on the play, saying that it is an insult to Ireland.' When we reached Abbey Street we found a great crowd assembled in the streets adjoining the theatre. Inside, the atmosphere was electric and there was suspense in the air, as though everyone in the auditorium expected a political revolution to break out. Instead of waiting quietly in their seats for the play to begin, many gathered together in groups talking excitedly, and I was struck, too, by the varying types I saw in the audience. In addition to the usual middle-class theatre-goers, there were numbers of workers, and here and there gentlemen and ladies in evening dress, and young men whose tousled hair and beards proclaimed them initiates of the Dublin

Scholars and Gypsies; An Autobiography (London: John Murray, 1963) pp.37–9.

Latin quarter. A wizened old man sitting next to me pointed out the literary and political celebrities as they took their places. 'See that long thin rake of a fellow, that's Best[1] the Librarian arguing with Dr R.M. Henry, one of the Belfast Home-Rulers. Next but two to him is a fine upstanding man with a beard: that's AE,[2] our Irish Buddha! Over there by himself is the victim of the evening, John Millington Synge. Every one of the Irish intellectuals are present, but it's not the play they've come to see, but to spy on one another.' I longed to ask the old man for an explanation for his cryptic words, but just then the lights dimmed and I heard a dismal gong sounding the knell as it seemed to me, and the curtain rose.

Although I tried very hard to concentrate upon the play it was impossible to hear the actors after the first few minutes because of the interruptions and disturbances which took place all over the auditorium. When these reached a climax, one[3] of the company advanced to the footlights and tried to appeal for silence. He said, as far as I could make out, that anyone in the audience who did not like the play was at liberty to get up and leave, but nobody left. Instead, pandemonium broke loose, and my wizened neighbour, whom I had considered an inoffensive old man, jumped to his feet shouting: 'Clear the decks! Down with Willie Fay!' And his shouts were taken up in chorus by the gallery. Then came shouts from the pit below and many started to sing the revolutionary song, *The West's asleep*.

While all this rumpus was going on the actors and actresses on the stage continued valiantly to act their parts, but they were puppets; I could see their lips move but hardly a word reached me. Paddy Tobin and I recognized some friends who were from Trinity College. They had come at the request of Lady Gregory's nephew with some other students to support the play. Seeing that the disturbances increased in the second act they thought the best way in which they could show their support of the play would be by singing *God Save the King* in chorus. Even today, when I look back at that fateful night in the history of the Irish National Theatre, I cannot imagine how such a crazy notion as singing the British National Anthem could have entered their heads. Instead of pouring oil on troubled waters they enraged the Irish patriots in the pit by singing what the latter considered a political song.

Paddy Tobin and I enjoyed ourselves immensely in the hullabaloo. Through the temptest of shouting and hissing we heard cries '*Sinn Fein Amhain*'[4] and 'kill the author', and from our seats at the side of the gallery we had a wonderful view of the milling mob in the pit and gallery. Then suddenly the doors of the auditorium opened and a posse of Dublin Metropolitan police entered, and many of the rowdy elements were cast out. We expected the burly giants to draw their batons and made ready to join the wild stampede, but there was a

momentary lull as another figure advanced to the footlights to speak
to the mob; but he was no more successful than his predecessor had
been in the first act, and his voice was drowned by catcalls and the
strident tones of toy trumpets. Those who thought the display of
force by the police would calm the rioters were mistaken, for Act III
of the play began amidst scenes of even greater chaos. As we were
unable to hear a single word of the play, and knowing that the fight
was spreading to the streets outside, we left our seats and mingled
with the crowd in the vestibule. Following Paddy during the interval I
managed to reach the back of the stage through a side door leading
into the lane, and we joined the actors and their supporters gathered
round Lady Gregory and J.M. Synge. While to me it seemed that all
the players were wringing their hands, tearing their hair and
running hither and thither, Lady Gregory stood at the door of the
Green Room as calm and collected as Queen Victoria about to open
a charity bazaar. Seeing Paddy Tobin and myself, she beckoned us
over and handed each of us a piece of the huge barmbrack which she
had baked at Coole and brought up to Dublin for the Abbey cast.
While we were munching our cake we observed the author, J.M.
Synge, mooning about among the actors like a lost soul. I had seen
him on various occasions in Kingstown, and when I passed him
striding along the Dalkey road swinging his stick I used to wonder
whether he was French or Austrian, for he had moustaches and a
little goatee or 'imperial'. When I saw him on the night of the Abbey
riot his face was pale and sunken, and he looked like a ghost of the
sun-tanned wanderer I had seen walking by the sea. I watched him
closely as he sat motionless through the dumb-show of his play,
amidst the rioting and insults of the mob, but not a trace of emotion
could I discern in his pale mask-like face that gazed unseeing at the
raging auditorium.

NOTES

Walter FitzWilliam Starkie (1894–1976) became a Fellow of Trinity College Dublin in
1920. During the War he was British Council representative in Madrid. He was also a
Director of the Abbey Theatre from 1926 to 1942 and a Professor-in-Residence at the
University of California in Los Angeles from 1961 to 1967. As a young man he had
studied music and played the violin all over Europe, using his skill to acquire
friendship of the gypsies, and to study their music and folklore. From this came *Raggle
Taggle* (1933), an account of his adventures in the Balkans. *Spanish Raggle Taggle* (1934),
Gypsy Folklore & Music (1935), *The Waveless Plain* (an Italian memoir; 1938), *In Sara's Tents*
(1953), *The Road to Santiago* (1957), and *Scholars & Gypsies* (autobiography; 1963) all reflect
this lifelong interest. In a letter to Lady Gerald Wellesley dated 30 June 1936, W.B.
Yeats described Starkie as a 'fat man ... who most years spends a couple of months
among gypsies in Spain, Austria, etc., playing his fiddle and escaping among the gypsy
women, according to one of the reviewers, "a fate worse than death" ... '

1. Dr Richard Irvine Best (1872–1959), distinguished Gaelic scholar and linguist who
was long associated with the National Library of Ireland. A well-known Dublin
character and friend of James Joyce and Oliver St John Gogarty, he appears under his

own name in *Ulysses* (the National Library episode). Until he arrived in London on 9 January 1903 Synge had met relatively few writers and artists. While he was very much a part of the W.B. Yeats–Lady Gregory circle in Ireland, his only other literary friends were Richard Best and Stephen MacKenna. It was in Paris where Synge first met Best, who had gone there to study Celtic.

2. AE [George Russell] (1867–1935), poet, painter, journalist and social thinker who played a considerable part in the Irish renaissance. He made the *Irish Homestead*, of which he was editor from 1906 to 1923, an important intellectual and literary journal. Although a passionate nationalist, he believed England and Ireland to be economically interdependent and therefore did not join in the Easter Rising of 1916. The most practical of economists and the most mystical of poets, he was the author of many volumes of essays and poetry. From 1923 to 1930 he was the editor of the *Irish Statesman*. Once, when he was exploring mysticism and theosophy in 1897, Synge went with AE to a meeting of the Theosophical Society. When the first three-year trial period of the Irish Literary Theatre closed and Edward Martyn and George Moore withdrew, Yeats, together with Lady Gregory and AE, in 1902 joined with the Fay brothers and their company.

3. William G. Fay.

4. 'Ourselves alone'.

Memories of Lady Gregory*

WILFRID SCAWEN BLUNT

14th March [1907].—Lady Gregory dined with me in Chapel Street. She gave me a long account of the row that took place at her Abbey Theatre, over the production of Synge's piece, 'The Playboy of the Western World.' The first night, she said, passed fairly well, with only a few hisses, but on the second night there was an organized opposition, and, fearing mischief, she sent for the police,[1] and afterwards there was a tumult every night of the week till the last performance, when the opponents of the play got tired of their noise. She considers, therefore, that she has won a victory, but fears the incident will have harmed her in the provinces, where the play is resented more than in Dublin. At Gort, her county town, the local council has boycotted her, forbidding the school children to attend her teas and entertainments, lest their morals should be corrupted. She is going abroad for a while with her son.

*   *   *

29th May [1907].—Chapel Street. Lady Gregory came to luncheon, in terrible trouble about her plays. She had gone to Italy to get away

*Extracted from *My Diaries; Being a Personal Narrative of Events 1888–1914*. Part 2, 1900–1914 (London: Martin Secker; New York: Alfred A. Knopf, 1921).

from the worry, with Yeats and her son, and had engaged to bring
out 'The Playboy' with other pieces at Oxford and in London but the
Censor interfered and she was telegraphed for to come back. Birrell,
however, to whom the case was referred, withdrew the Censor's
opposition. I am of opinion she would do better to withdraw the
play, but she has others to consult and Yeats is obstinate.

   1st June.—Newbuildings. Lady Gregory is in worse trouble than
ever. The Editor of the 'Freeman' has written threatening her with
new displeasure if she persists with 'The Playboy' in England, and I
fear her theatre will be altogether boycotted. I advise her to submit to
Irish opinion, but though she admits that it was a mistake to produce
the play, she says it is too late now to withdraw it. The worst of it is
that she is already boycotted personally on account of it at Coole, the
Local Council forbidding the school-children to go to her house, or
even to accept cakes or presents of any kind from her; it is the Sinn
Fein that has done it.

   She told me an interesting fact of past history connected with
Layard's[2] life at Constantinople and his secret despatch against the
Sultan which Granville published. The Sultan's mind had been set
against Layard's by someone and, at an audience, though they had
been close friends, Abdul Hamid behaved in such a way as to show
that he feared Layard would attack him. This was the occasion of the
secret despatch being written. It cost Layard the peerage he aspired
to, for Lord Salisbury[3] had promised it, but the Queen refused, saying
that no ambassador ought to write in such terms of the sovereign to
whom he was accredited. Lady Gregory knows this, as Sir William
(her husband) was intermediary in the affair of the peerage.

*   *   *

   5th June (Sunday) [1910].—Lady Gregory and Yeats came down to
dine and sleep, Yeats in good form, telling a number of excellent
stories at dinner. He said that the three persons he had known who
had most impressed him with their power were William Morris,[4]
Henley,[5] and Madame Blavatsky.[6] He had gone on one occasion with
Oscar Wilde to call on Henley. Oscar did not before know Henley,
and put out all his most brilliant talk to captivate him and succeeded
in doing so, while Henley said nothing. Both professed themselves
afterwards much pleased with the other's wit.

   Lady Gregory is bringing out her new three-act play, 'The Image',[7]
at the Court Theatre. They have also Synge's 'Deirdre' on their list,
but they say it is not successful. Yeats tells me he makes only about
£30 a year by the sale of his poetry. He is an extremely pleasant
fellow, and has a more prosperous look, and is fatter and rosier than
formerly. Lady Gregory has been the making of him.

NOTES

Wilfrid Scawen Blunt (1840–1922), English poet; traveller in Asia Minor, Arabia, and North Africa; breeder of Arab horses; opponent of colonialism; and supporter of Irish Home Rule. In November 1892, eight months after Sir William Gregory's death, Blunt notes in his diary that his friend Margot Tennant, the future Mrs Asquith, is planning a woman's magazine. 'They are in straits for a political leader-writer, and I suggested Lady Gregory.' The magazine did not materialise, but the suggestion shows her already anxious to be considered a professional writer.

1. Yeats was absent from Ireland for the debut of *The Playboy*; he was lecturing in Scotland. While Lady Gregory resolutely kept the play running against organised interruption, Yeats hurried back to Dublin and arranged a debate in the Abbey Theatre on Monday, 4 February 1907, following the week's performances.

2. Sir Austen Henry Layard (1817–94), English archaeologist whose Mesopotamian excavations did much to reveal the ancient civilisation and wonders of Babylonia and Assyria. During his later career in government and diplomacy, Layard served in Parliament, became Under-Secretary of Foreign Affairs, and was appointed Chief Commissioner of Works, Privy Councillor and Ambassador at Istanbul.

3. The British Prime Minister.

4. William Morris (1834–96), English designer, craftsman, poet and early socialist, whose designs for the decorative arts revolutionised Victorian taste and whose diverse activities were all inspired by a high moral seriousness that endowed his work with dignity, a sense of purpose, and a virile freshness of approach.

5. William Ernest Henley (1849–1903), English poet, critic and editor who in his journals introduced the early work of many of the great English writers of the 1890s.

6. Helena Petrovna Blavatsky (1831–91), Russian spiritualist, author, and co-founder of the Theosophical Society to promote Theosophy, an occult philosophical-religious system largely derived from Hindu writings, whose followers believe in a pantheistic evolutionary process integrating deity, cosmos and self.

7. *The Image* was first performed at the Abbey Theatre on 11 November 1909.

The Comedy Spirit of Ireland*

Imagine a grandmother leaving behind a christening cake for her latest granddaughter, dashing across Ireland in an automobile from Galway to Queenstown[1] through night and fog because the railroad men seize an opportune season to strike, catching an ocean liner after many mishaps, with little or no time to spare; rattling off on the keys of a typewriter the rough draft of a play in mid-ocean, and arriving smiling and unperturbed to face a score of photographers and interviewers—imagine all that, and there's Lady Gregory.

The representative of the comedy spirit in the group of

Sunday Herald (Boston) (1 Oct 1911) Magazine section.

enthusiastic young dramatists in the great Irish literary revival of which William Butler Yeats is the leading exponent, Lady Gregory laughs at difficulties, and to know this is to appreciate in a large measure how the folk-lore movement has achieved its striking success in a scant dozen years.

Arriving in Boston Friday morning—it is her first visit to this country—she at once took up her portion of the burden of supervising, with Mr. Yeats, the production of the repertory of dramas which are being presented by the Irish Players at the Plymouth Theatre.[2] Although several of her own comedies are among those which are being produced for the first time in this city, her chief interest is in J.M. Synge's 'The Playboy of the Western World,' about which a storm of controversy has raged ever since it first made its appearance on the stage of the Abbey Theatre in Dublin.

That she has not come with any elaborate defence of the 'Playboy', as she abbreviates the title, Lady Gregory makes haste to explain. She is here to let it speak for itself as an artistic masterpiece. A 'great work of fantasy,' she characterizes it, adding with a smile, 'I will admit that I have some sympathy for the honest objectors to it.' Of the group of men who tried to drive it from the stage at the start with tin horns and trumpets she is charitably silent.

Beginning her work as a dramatist at a period of life when most literary aspirants are thinking of retiring on royalties, Lady Gregory has been the soul of energy and ceaseless activity. From a quiet retreat at her home in Coole Park, Gort, in Galway, she threw herself into the thick of the movement for an Irish national theatre and has remained in the forefront as author, managing director and propagandist. For here there has been at least as much hard work as glory, although there has been a full mead of the latter, for the pit, 'our pit' idolizes her with a loyal tribute of laughter.

THE REAL PIONEER

'How did I become identified with the movement? I didn't become identified. Mr. Yeats and I started it, I think. We were the movement. I was a great admirer of Mr. Yeats's verse plays and began first by writing scenarios, because I distrusted my ability to write dialogue. I did several scenarios for Douglas Hyde,[3] and it was in that form that I gave 'The Workhouse Ward'[4] to him. He suggested that I write the play myself. When I took up the work I found the dialogue came more easily than I expected, and I have been writing plays ever since.'

That Lady Gregory has been working to some purpose those who have had the privilege of hearing not only 'The Workhouse Ward,' but 'Hyacinth Halvey'[5] and 'The Rising of the Moon'[6] as well, are willing to testify. 'It's a friendly satire,' says the author of mirth provoking comedies. The too-serious is not a part of her work, as she has explained: 'All the young writers are so busy writing tragedy that I shall have to go on, as I am the only one old enough to laugh.'

Previous to her interest in Mr. Yeats, Lady Gregory had a passionate devotion to the old Gaelic legends and the Gaelic revival in general. She made numerous translations of the folk tales of Ireland, and from these imbibed much of the 'folk spirit' which has been a basic principle of the new drama. To Mr. Yeats chiefly has been given the interpretation of that spirit in the mystical, fiery nuances of lyrical poetry among the group of enthusiasts surrounding him.

Lady Gregory has endeavored to evoke the selfsame spirit in modern terms, taking as her exponents the life and speech of the Green Isle as it is today.

'The folk spirit,' she says, 'is with the people today. It is there in their very life; it is present in their everyday talk; it is strong in their picturesque phrases. Both Synge and I have sought to reproduce the beautiful rhythm which the whole peasantry speak. No. I have not consciously sought after that speech. I have lived my whole life among the people, and their modes of expression come naturally to me. I find it in talking with my tenants, with workmen, with tramps, with beggar women. I find it everywhere about my own home.'

'But what have you to say of the charge that the spirit is wholly pagan?' Lady Gregory was asked.

'It's a humbug,' replied her ladyship with a smile. 'You see I was christened, confirmed and married. I just left Ireland before the christening of my granddaughter, and I left behind a big christening cake. Am I not a good Christian?'

Of her own plays Lady Gregory has little to say, but of the plays that her coworkers have produced and the success of them she has enthusiastic commendation. The result accomplished by the National Theatre is a theme upon which she likes to talk.

EARLY DIFFICULTIES

It was no easy matter to get that theatre under way, in the first place. Three others had a virtual monopoly of production in Dublin, and it was necessary to have the law altered before the new drama could secure a place in which to get a hearing. Then it became necessary to find an audience.

On that head, however, there proved to be little difficulty, for from the start the people seemed to appreciate the new literature. 'Our Pit,' as Lady Gregory speaks of those who occupy the cheaper seats in the theatre in Dublin, and represent the masses, has proved appreciative from the beginning.

'It has always been easy to fill our pit,' she says, 'and we have always been assured of an intelligent hearing from that part of the house. There has never been anything that we have produced which has proved too mystical or too poetical for them, despite the belief to the contrary.'

With Mr. Yeats, Lady Gregory has been active in selecting the plays produced, and as a result they have made few errors in judgment. No play that has been refused by them has yet made its appearance elsewhere. And in the selection of plays not the least arduous labor in connection with the theatre has been done.

The success of the new movement has developed a large number of aspiring young authors who have gone to see the drama in Dublin and returned home to write. Some of the plays submitted have been mere copies of the more successful productions, but others have shown marked promise.

The labor of reading and selecting has fallen largely upon Mr. Yeats and Lady Gregory. At times the piece offered has had decided merit, but glaring defects. It has often been necessary to accept the offerings as scenarios, and to do the actual writing as a whole or to rewrite in part. Besides, there was advice to be given, suggestions to be made as to how the original draft might be improved, and a mass of other details to be attended to.

THE GOOD FRUITS

As a result of the untiring zeal of the leaders, however, there has grown up a successful group of playwrights, imbued with the new spirit, and now capable in technique as well as fluent of ideas. The supply is immense, and no play which is not fitted for repertory is accepted.

Despite the fact that there are so many young writers in the field Lady Gregory has not ceased her activity as a dramatist and on the Cymric[7] on her way to Boston she found time to complete a rough draft of a new comedy to be known as 'McDonough's Wife,'[8] detailing the adventures of one McDonough, a piper. In her spare hours she has learned to use a typewriter, and it was through the machine that McDonough came into being.

Her departure from her home for Boston was not without its excitement. The strike on the Irish railroads had tied up traffic and it was necessary to borrow an automobile from Lord Gough, a neighbor. The English chauffeur was unfamiliar with the roads between Gort and Queenstown, and missed his way several times, finally missing Queenstown by 10 miles. Several punctures added to the excitement and the petrol gave out when the car with Lady Gregory was within half a mile of its destination. But Lady Gregory caught the boat.

Although she confesses to grandmotherhood, she seems scarcely beyond middle life, and there is youth in her smile which makes one forget the gray hair smoothed away from the forehead. Her eyes, keen and dark, light up with a quizzical expression as she talks. She gives the impression of one who has found and will find much that is pleasant in the things about her.

Of her George Bernard Shaw, an ardent admirer of her work, said not long ago:

'If ever there was a person doomed from the cradle to write for the stage, to break through every social obstacle to get to the stage—nay, to invent and create a theatre if no theatre existed—that person is the author 'Hyacinth Halvey,' of 'The Workhouse Ward' and of 'The Rising of the Moon.' Her plays never fail to do the one thing which we all demand from a play, which is not, as stupid people say, to amuse us (though Lady Gregory's plays are extremely amusing), but to take us out of ourselves, out of London and out of the stuffy theatre while we are listening to them.'

Lady Gregory is the widow of Sir William Gregory, former Governor of Ceylon, and appears in the peerage as Isabella Augusta.

NOTES

In 1911, The Abbey Theatre Company, known as The Irish Players, made their first American tour, which was so successful that they were obliged to remain in the United States from September 1911 to March 1912. The tour opened in Boston on 23 September. The critical reaction was generally enthusiastic, but on 4 October an ominous letter by Dr J.T. Gallagher appeared in the *Boston Post*. However, aside from a mild disturbance on the opening night, sporadic hissing at *The Playboy of the Western World*, and an attempt to have the censor ban the plays, the Boston run was successfully concluded with no demonstrations in the theatre. From Boston the Company went to Providence, where a deputation of Irish-Americans demanded that another play be substituted for *The Playboy*. Lady Gregory, who accompanied the players throughout, refused. In New Haven, the Chief of Police, acting as the official censor, attended an afternoon rehearsal and demanded that a list of cuts he had noted be made in Synge's play before it could go on in the evening. The Company encountered the first organised opposition by the Catholic Church in Washington. Here, the Irish Players were condemned from the altar by priests of Irish descent. In New York, the notoriety given by the riots brought people to the theatre in great numbers. The plays were also a success in Philadelphia, though the entire Company was arrested under a law enacted the year previous on the eve of Sarah Bernhardt's visit, forbidding 'immoral or indecent plays'. After Philadelphia, the Company went to Pittsburgh, Indianapolis, and Chicago. The farther west the Company went, the less violent the disturbances. In spite of the resolution of Irish-Americans in Chicago that they did not want the play presented there, and a threatening letter with a picture of a coffin and pistol which declared that Lady Gregory would 'never see the hills of Connemara again', as she was about to meet her death, *The Playboy* ended its Chicago run in such peace that Lady Gregory 'nearly fell asleep'.

1. Now Dun Laoghaire.

2. See 'Plymouth Theatre', *Boston Evening Record* (26 Sep 1911).

3. Douglas Hyde (1860–1949), distinguished Gaelic scholar and writer and first President of Eire. He was the outstanding figure in the struggle for the preservation and extension of the Irish language from 1893, when he founded the Gaelic League,

until 1922, when the founding of the Irish Free State accorded the Irish language equal status with English. See Lester Connor, 'The Importance of Douglas Hyde to the Irish Literary Renaissance', *Modern Irish Literature: Essays in Honor of William York Tindall*, ed. Raymond J. Porter and James D. Brophy (New Rochelle, New York: Iona College Press, 1972) pp. 95–114; Dominic Daly, *The Young Douglas Hyde: The Dawn of the Irish Revolution & Renaissance* (Dublin: Irish University Press, 1974); and Diarmuid Coffey, *Douglas Hyde, President of Ireland* (Dublin: Talbot Press, 1938). On the collaboration between Lady Gregory and Douglas Hyde see Elizabeth Coxhead, 'Collaboration—Hyde', *Lady Gregory; A Literary Portrait*, 2nd ed., revised and enlarged (London: Secker & Warburg, 1966) pp. 108–11.

4. *The Workhouse Ward* opened at the Abbey Theatre on 20 April 1908. The genesis of the play is mentioned in the chapter called 'Play-Writing' in Lady Gregory's *Our Irish Theatre* (London: Putnam, 1914). The notion of the two old people kept alive by their joy in a quarrel was suggested to Lady Gregory by an incident in Gort Workhouse.

5. *Hyacinth Halvey* was first presented at the Abbey Theatre on 19 February 1906.

6. *The Rising of the Moon* was first produced at the Abbey Theatre on 9 March 1907.

7. The steamer.

8. The first night of *MacDonough's Wife* was at the Abbey Theatre on 11 January 1912.

A Lively Discussion over the 'Irish Plays'*

There is widespread discussion in Boston and vicinity over a series of plays now being produced at the Plymouth Theatre. The *Post* has been in receipt of numerous letters, many in protest and many in approval of these productions.

Prominent Americans, of Irish birth or of Irish descent, have condemned, in the strongest terms, the remarkable plays which the Irish poet, William Butler Yeats, and the gifted Irish authoress, Lady Gregory, have introduced to Boston; others, equally prominent and patriotic, have lauded and praised the plays unstintedly.

Discussion is still at fever heat, and the great question naturally arises: Which of these two factions is right? The *Sunday Post* is enabled to give herewith the views of a number[1] of Boston's most prominent citizens of Irish extraction.

The question at issue is whether these plays give a fair representation of life and conditions in Ireland. This seems to be an entirely legitimate subject for public discussion, and the *Post*, as usual, prints herewith both sides of the controversy.

*Extracted from the *Sunday Post* (Boston) (8 Oct 1911).

STIR UP DISCUSSION

When the Irish players arrived in Boston, barely two weeks ago, they little imagined the tempest they would stir up. What are the lines that are objected to?

What are the scenes objected to?

What are the objections, and what are the defences advanced?

The Irish players, fresh from a season of prosperity at their little theatre in Dublin, the Abbey Theatre, arrived in Boston heralded as the revivers of the old folk-spirit of poetry and drama in Ireland.

They came over, the company of actors—acknowledged splendid even by many opposed to the plays—and with them came William Butler Yeats, the poet, and Lady Gregory, the Irish poetess and authoress.

THREE PLAYS

They produced three plays, among others, in their first week— 'Birthright'[2] by T.C. Murray, 'Hyacinth Halvey' by Lady Gregory, and 'The Shadow of the Glen'[3] by J.M. Synge.

These three plays aroused some of Boston's prominent playgoers to a height of indignation, where they felt that withdrawal should be immediately demanded. They felt that the plays gave distorted views of Irish life: that in many cases the people pictured had no existence; that the characters were either abnormal, vicious, immoral, deceitful, cowardly or blasphemous.

On the other hand many prominent Irish-Americans, quite patriotic, found the plays to be admirable: admirably acted, quite true to life, absolutely inoffensive and human in portrayal of the characters.

POINTS OF VIEW

That such a divergence of opinion can exist is remarkable. Nothing but a careful individual study of the plays can show the source of the various points of view.

Mr. Yeats, the poet, declares that the criticisers of the plays are all in the wrong.[4] He believes that his players are not making the slightest attempt to malign the Irish people, to misrepresent them or to distort their characteristics in any way.

BY LADY GREGORY

In an interview for the *Sunday Post* Lady Gregory said:

I think it quite natural that some should misunderstand our intentions. We do not come to portray Irish people. We are simply giving plays, the scenes of which happen to be laid amongst the humble folk, who form the most picturesque and distinctly national part of our population.

I am sure that a little more familiarity with our ideals and our intentions will show the critics their errors—errors natural and easily forgiven, as due to an excess of sensitiveness and a lack of close study of our purposes.

NOTES

1. Participants in the 'Discussion' included Dr James T. Gallagher, W.B. Yeats, Dr T.J. Dillon, Mary Boyle O'Reilly, Michael Maynes, Katherine R. Walsh, Margaret Foley, Felix W. McGettrick, Dr Edward F. Timmins, Mary A. Cavanagh, Congressman O'Connell, Mayor Fitzgerald, William A. Leahy, Mark H. Crehan, W.T.A. Fitzgerald, James F. Cavanagh, Thomas F. Molloy, and Thomas O. M'Enaney.

2. The first performance of *Birthright* was at the Abbey Theatre on 27 October 1910.

3. *The Shadow of the Glen* had its première at the Molesworth Hall on 8 October 1903.

4. See also 'Yeats Replies to His Critics; Defends Irish Plays Being Produced Here', *Boston Post* (5 Oct 1911); 'Yeats Defends "The Playboy"', *Boston Herald*, (12 Oct 1911); and 'Mr. Yeats Explains', *Boston Evening Transcript* (13 Oct 1911).

A Repertory Theatre*

Now and again there is a sigh or a rumor of sadness among the people in this city—among those, that is, who have any real interest in the theatre, be it that of a professional, an amateur or a connoissour. The sigh is for a more earnest theatre, a more flavorsome theatre; for plays that were written because the writers had to write them or burst with the repression, and acted by players who have gone on the stage because they had something in them that drew them to the footlights with an irresistible current. Those who care to have a theatre which can offer them these things have a plan—that is, a dream—of how to accomplish it. But every one tells them it is impossible. History says it is practical and that it has been done many times. It is merely the founding and maintaining of a repertory theatre. But this is one of the things that 'cannot be done in New York.' The phrase is a popular one, and has preceded many things in other departments of life that now exist here and seem to be reasonably well rooted—the traffic squad, for one instance, and the subway, for another. Both of these things 'could not be done in New York,' according to the deciders of the public rate ten or fifteen

New York Daily Tribune (26 Nov 1911) Part V.

years ago. Now the thing that cannot exist in New York is a repertory theatre, and the cry is so persistent and is getting so much louder day by day that it must be almost time for one to be started.

That a repertory theatre can exist elsewhere has been proved by the Irish players, or, more particularly, by their directors, William Butler Yeats and Lady Gregory. Lady Gregory is in New York now, devotedly attending every performance of the company at Maxine Elliott's Theatre, and to hear her tell of the Irish players—who they are, whence they came, what this whole unique national play movement represents in Ireland—is like reading from old books about the theatre, when acting was dear to the hearts of the people and was called an art.

The whole movement started, according to Lady Gregory, in the desire of a few persons to express something that was in them. It did not start in some one's formulated plan to found a repertory theatre, nor was it necessary to scour the country to find playwrights, plays and actors, and force them into an inharmonious organization. The movement simply grew. Yeats was one of the principal ones.

He called on Lady Gregory in London one day—she has it recorded in her diary. 'He was seething with plays and plans,' she wrote. He counselled long and often with her, and as a result they went over to Dublin and collected a little company of English actors to produce one or two of Yeats's plays. The plays attracted attention, because they were simple and because they went down to the people, instead of exploiting society. As George Moore put it, they were a change from the plays in which 'a gentleman in evening clothes and gold shirt studs tries to persuade a lady in silk dresses to leave her husband.' They attempted to strike a note that was distinctively Irish. Many persons who were interested in the theatre gathered. Other young dramatists of something the same ideas as Yeats submitted plays, Irish actors applied for the privilege of acting in them, and finally Miss Horniman[1] appeared and offered money enough to found a national theatre in Dublin. That, in brief, was the beginning.

'It began to grow clear to us then,' said Lady Gregory, 'that we were doing something more significant that just conducting a personal theatre and producing a more elemental kind of play. It began to dawn upon us that both plays and acting had, in a way, gone unconsciously down into national traits and discovered a poetry and a sense of things that were distinctively Irish. After that we went more deliberately to work to develop this tendency as far as we were able.

'We advertised for Irish players, and took a number who were young and had never acted anywhere. These we trained to do as we wanted them to.

'Last year I saw the Sicilian players and was deeply interested in their use of gesture. So wonderfully sensitive are these people's hands to form and action that their plays could have been understood by watching their gestures alone. The directors of that company had realized the natural trait of the people and had developed it into an art that was full of meaning.

'In the same way we realized that the Irish are not light and graceful of movement and quick of manner and action, so we did not try to cultivate these traits in them. We realized that they had beautiful voices naturally, so we let gesticulation count for very little and developed the subtle shades of the voice and depended on this vocal power for dramatic effect.

'Our theme, since we began consciously to have one, has been to find what was essentially natural in the Irish people and characteristic of them and to develop those things to their utmost power of growth.

'The outcome of this effort has been perhaps the founding of a school of acting in Ireland. We have now a place near the Abbey Theatre in Dublin where we are training young men and women who will gradually come into the company. Mr. Yeats is there now working with them. You see, we have only fifteen players; in fact, five of those are merely substitutes who are comparatively new to the company. We want at least thirty players, for we have a repertory of eighty plays already, and besides we want to be able while we have a company travelling to have one also at Dublin. It is not fair to have our theatre there empty for so many weeks for so long a time as we have spent over here this fall. We plan to come to America again next year with some of the verse dramas, plays that we were afraid to attempt before we were known here. Then London is constantly sending for us, and we want to be able to run over there now and again, yet always leaving enough players behind to play continually at home.

'The dramatic season in Dublin, you know, is much longer than it is in New York. We have only six weeks' holiday in the summer time there. During all the rest of the year the playhouse is open. This continuous work in itself makes it necessary for us to have a larger company so that the members of it will not be overstrained.

'In connection with the rest of the movement, and naturally as a result of it, many new dramatists have appeared—young men with unfulfilled and unaccomplished dreams. They are growing with the movement and writing better every year. We are constantly reading their plays and encouraging them, accepting what is good. We do not accept anything that we do not consider good enough to add to our repertory for constant production. We produce nothing, you see, just for a run. What we play we intend to make permanent, that is, to standardize.'

'And yourself, Lady Gregory, the Abbey Theatre has been an outlet for your plays?'

'Oh, my plays,' she smiled. 'I took to writing them to fill a need. The young men who were writing were all so serious. They were writing tragedies. I wrote my comedies to lighten the programmes so that audiences would not have only the heavier works to see. I have kept on writing them till the younger ones should grow old enough to see that life had a brighter side.' Lady Gregory smiled reminiscently. 'Now,' she went on, 'I am so interested in playwriting, especially my folk dialect plays, that I suppose I shall go right along with them. I wrote one coming over on the steamer to America.'

'Are you not afraid of losing one of the players through the tempting offers which are being made to them to stay in America?' she was asked.

'I think we shall return as we came,' she answered. 'Several members of the company received very large offers in London last year, but they all refused. I think they realize that their strength lies in their unity and their interdependence on one another. They are almost like a family, anyway. They never have acted in any other company, you know. Their experience is wholly limited to their experience with each other and under our management, and they seem to feel that they are a little community of interest that must hang together, at least so long as they wish to be players: Then, too, we are all working out something together, and the members of the company are as much interested in their work as the playwrights and directors are in theirs. Perhaps that is why we have been able to do what we have as quickly and as well as we have—we all work together.'

NOTE

1. Annie Elizabeth Frederika Horniman (1860–1937), English theatre manager and patron, was one of the first to organize and encourage the modern repertory theatre movement. She built and managed the Abbey Theatre in Dublin for the Irish National Theatre Society (1904), and bought and managed the Gaiety Theatre in Manchester (1908–21). See James W. Flannery, *Miss Annie F. Horniman and the Abbey Theatre* (Dublin: The Dolmen Press, 1970).

A Rousing Playboy Riot*

There was a ruction in Dublin when J.M. Synge's *The Playboy of the Western World* was first produced there, and in this country there have been many rumbling resolutions from assembled Irish societies since the Irish Players began to play here, but no theatre riot of modern times could approach that enacted Monday night at the Maxine Elliott Theatre, where the Synge play was announced for first production in New York.

When the curtain rose there were signs of uneasiness among the audience, which did not seem greatly to differ from the gatherings that had previously seen the Irish Players.

But the play had hardly commenced when a potato swept through the air from the gallery and smashed against the wings. Then came a shower of vegetables that pattered against the scenery and made the actors duck and run for shelter.

A potato struck Miss MaGee,[1] but she glared defiance. Men rose in the gallery and balcony and cried out to stop the performance. In the orchestra several men stood up and menaced the actors.

'Go on with the play,' came an order from the stage-manager, and the players took their places and began to speak their lines.

The tumult broke out more violently than before, and more vegetables came sailing through the air and rolled about the stage. Then began the fall of capsules that broke as they hit the stage. They were filled with asafœtida, and their odor was suffocating and nauseating.

One of the theatre employees had run to the street to ask for police protection at the outset of the disturbance but the response was so slow that the ushers and the doortenders undertook to suppress the riot, throwing out men indiscriminately, for the excitement was so great that real offenders could not be told from persons who were merely alarmed.

The Broadway crowds soon filled Thirty-ninth Street in the vicinity of the theatre. Soon a hundred policemen got to work, some of them being in plain clothes, and disturbers were ejected in no gentle way. All who fell into police hands protested at the 'outrage' of ejection, and pandemonium still reigned.

New York Dramatic Mirror, LXVI (29 Nov 1911) pp. 7, 11.

The play went on spasmodically, in spite of the noise and confusion, and when the first act was finished an announcement was made that it would be repeated, so that all present could see it. The scenes were shifted again and the stage setting at the beginning rearranged, and then the players came on and began again at the beginning.

And still the missiles flew. By this time the police were so thick that there was no longer danger of more than sporadic cases of violence. But through the first act again and through all of the other acts there were still cries of protest and still vegetables were aimed at the players. One man threw an old Waterbury watch that struck one of the actors and fell jingling to the stage.

During the trouble Lady Gregory talked to the reporters. She said: 'I wish the men who threw the things on the stage had taken better aim, for I can't believe that they intended to hit anybody. Miss MaGee would have been injured if her thick hair had not protected her. She was struck on the head, but fortunately she escaped without hurt.

'The play was first produced in January, 1907, in Dublin, but we had no trouble like this. The police put a stop to it. The second time it was put on in Dublin the disturbers were put out right at the beginning. We had some trouble in Boston and in Providence, but nothing like this.'

George C. Tyler, manager of the Irish Players, said: 'We will keep the play on and play it through if it takes us all night.'

When the actors had ended the performance, for which many remained, though little could be heard, the police had made ten prisoners.

NOTE

1. Ethne Magee, who played the part of Pegeen.

How Ireland Turned from Politics to Playwriting*

When did the new Irish literary movement begin?

The moment Parnell died.

That moment, according to Lady Gregory, was the sharply defined beginning of a new era for Ireland. Usually it is rather hard to tell the exact time when a movement in art or politics had its origin, but this is an exception. Up to that time Ireland had been engrossed in politics and the question of subsistence. Throughout the nineteenth century she had had no real literature of her own. The Irishmen who wrote novels during that century merely skimmed the surface of things, and anyway, the novel is not the natural Irish mode of expression.

That mode is the drama. It is through the drama that the Irish genius naturally finds expression, as other nations find theirs in romance or lyric poetry.

But with the death of Parnell came an end to the absorbing topic that had occupied all Ireland's energies for so many years. The literary instinct, necessarily dormant because its expression would have found no audience, awoke, and turned itself toward the drama as a mode of expression. And now the new Ireland is beginning—the Ireland that thinks replaces the Ireland that merely fights.

All this is a free—perhaps too free—summary of the impression gained by a *Sunday Times* reporter, who asked Lady Gregory last week to tell him the meaning of such movements as are represented by the Irish players now in New York.

What she had to say was said back of the stage in the Maxine Elliott Theatre. So near were the players that sometimes what she said was half drowned by their voices. They were playing Synge's *Playboy of the Western World,* and 'in front' an enthusiastic audience was breaking in with storms of applause. The rioting bartenders and clerks of Monday night had either been cowed by the uncompromising attitude of the Irish-American police or had been shamed by the disapproval of the real Irishmen who have so heartily supported their countrymen in the effort to produce these Irish plays.

The New York Times Magazine (3 Dec 1911) p. 5.

It seemed amusing to think of this outbreak of Irish 'patriotism' in view of the thick Irish atmosphere that hung about the theatre. Most of the rioters talk with an accent in which, whatever faint remains there may be of Irish, are over-laid heavily by New Yorkese. But everybody connected with the Irish Players speaks with the genuine Irish brogue, from manager down. You can cut the brogue with a knife as you go in. It is funny to think of the pseudo-Irishmen outside, who haven't seen Ireland for years, if they ever saw it, demonstrating their noisy patriotism at the expense of genuine Irishmen and Irish girls fresh from the old sod, who are really trying to do something for Ireland—for the new Ireland.

'Two of those who were arrested for rioting on Tuesday night,' said Lady Gregory, 'were Englishmen, who didn't like the reference to khaki-clad cut-throats. And that reminds me of an experience we had with the English censor when we took *The Playboy of the Western World* to London. The censor, you know, was so very particular that he wouldn't pass *The Showing Up of Blanco Posnet*.[1]

'He struck out only one sentence in *The Playboy*. We ourselves had struck out a good many in the beginning, but the only one he cut was this about the khaki cut-throats. He wrote us a note, saying, 'This expression must be omitted, together with any other that may be considered derogatory to his Majesty's forces.'

'So every one, you see, looks out for his own side of the question.'

And Lady Gregory laughed happily at the idea that the English had objected to the play as too Irish and the Irish had objected to it as anti-Irish. It is pleasant to hear Lady Gregory laugh. It is a low laugh which expresses real enjoyment, and her smile is an irradiating flash of joy in a mobile face that is full of Irish humour—the humour so sadly lacking in her pseudo-Irish assailants. The way in which her brown eyes light up adds considerably to the infectious fun of that laugh.

The reporter asked her to tell him the origin of the movement of which she and W. Butler Yeats are the leading exponents.

'About twelve years ago,' she answered, 'Mr. Yeats and I started the Irish Literary Theatre. It was a modest enterprise enough; a week in each year was given up to the acting of Irish plays by Irish writers, and to produce them we got a company over from London. The actors were chosen by Mr. Yeats and Mr. Martin [sic] and Mr. George Moore.

'That experiment lasted three years.'

'In other words, there were just three weeks of this Irish drama?' asked the reporter.

'Yes,' assented Lady Gregory, 'a week in each year for three years. It attracted a great deal of interest. The plays were Mr Yeats's *Countess Cathleen* and a play[2] by George Moore and one[3] by Edward Martin.

'Then the experiment came to an end and we started again, this

time with the Irish Players. We found that there were a great many
Irish actors on the stage, but they had been trained in England and
they had no particular desire, or ability either, to play Irish plays, any
more than English plays. They had lost their nationality, as so many
Irishmen do who go to England.'

'Then you trained amateurs?'

'Amateurs is not the word. People look upon amateurs as persons
of leisure, rather dilettante, whereas these were people who did it for
love of the work. They came to us very young, and for awhile they
played for nothing. Then, of course, as we prospered a little more, we
needed actors whose whole time we could command, and they were
regularly paid.'

'But what was the inspiration of the movement? When and how
did Ireland turn to this mode of literary expression?'

'I should trace it back to the moment after Parnell's death. For
twelve years before he died the whole imagination of Irishmen was
taken up with the land war. There was nothing else thought of but
the farmer and the landlord, the one pitted against the other.

'And every one's eyes were drawn towards the English Parliament,
and some patriots were dreaming of a nation once again; and there
was no Irish literature written. There were a few novels by people of
leisure, but they didn't express Ireland in any way.

'Well, you see, after Parnell's death his party broke up; it was
pretty much like the disbanding of an army. They had lost the
keenness for the fight. The party broke up into two sections, and
neither quite knew whom it was hitting at.

'And then the imagination of Irishmen, especially in Ireland,
being set free, looked about for something to pitch on; and that
imagination, at least among young Irishmen, turned to this dramatic
form rather than to novels or poems. That, I think, is the origin of it.

'At the same time Dr Douglas Hyde formed his Gaelic League, for
the purpose of reviving the Irish language; and although we don't
use the Irish language in our plays, still the excitement caused by its
revival, the discovery that there was a great deal of legend and
culture and song-making still among the people, rather send writers
back to the life of the country itself, instead of looking for an
inspiration outside.

'It was so it happened with Mr. Synge. He was living abroad, not
doing anything of any value in literature; and then he came back,
partly moved by this new excitement, and lived there in the extreme
West for a part of every year, and wandered about, and there he got
that wonderful language that he uses in his verse-plays, and also got
his material.

'Of course all the material is changed when it passes through an
imaginative mind; it changes a little with the temperament of the

writer. There is something of harshness and gloom in his writings, perhaps a slight morbidity, which casual critics put down to French influence, but which I think was due to the shadow of his early death.[4]

'He was never in good health. At that time he had only a very few years of writing before him. He was 35 years old when he died.[5]

'This play of his was attacked when he was living, and we stood by him. Naturally, you may see, it is extremely unlikely that we should give it up after his death. It is unlikely we should do less for him when he was out of our sight than we had done for him living.'

She said it with the utmost simplicity, but with a look in her eyes that told volumes in explanation of the resolute way in which she and the Irish Players have faced down mobs and stood by their guns in their undaunted presentation of the dead poet's play. There is a drama there, too, even if it never should be written. Loyalty is not gone from Ireland yet. The dead man guides the production of his plays, in the midst of daunting difficulties, guides it through those who hold his memory dear, and mobs cannot frighten them.

'You spoke,' said the reporter, 'of Mr Synge's getting the language he uses from his observation of the people on the west coast. Surely they don't speak as poetically as he represents them?

'They do, yes,' answered Lady Gregory. 'Of course, he has heightened it a good deal, but they have a beautiful dialect there, and they have on an extraordinary ear. The Gaelic language itself depends very much on ear and rhythm, and when those who are thinking in Gaelic speak in English they get the same rhythm.

'You may see it in my plays, where I have written in dialect, though much less than you will see it in Mr Synge's. They have also a repetition of phrase, which they use just as the Hebrew poets do.

'The Hebrew poet will say, "The heavens declare the glory of God, the firmament showeth His handiwork." You see the effect produced by the repetition of the idea in the second part of the sentence. So an Irish peasant will say, "She is dead and she is not living, she is buried and gone to the grave." For the sake of the sound the idea is emphasized and repeated.

'Of course Synge heightened it; one does in writing. It undergoes some change in passing through the mind of a writer. Synge made a study of it. I had used it before him, in my translation from the Irish epics—those epics which Mr Roosevelt has written about.'

The reporter asked whether the original intention of the new Irish dramatists had been merely to express Irish life, or to establish a new school of writing.

'I don't think anybody sets out with a plan of that sort,' said Lady Gregory. 'All I wanted was to see Mr. Yeats's beautiful verse-plays acted in Ireland and to hear his words spoken on the stage. Then I happened to write my comedies, not with any such purpose as you mention, but because it is necessary to have some comedies as a relief or change from listening to verse.

'It is a beautiful thing to have plays written that are not likely to be taken by the ordinary commercial theatre. We take immense pains with the writing of them. Mr. Yeats writes and rewrites to get them what he desires them to be, and so do I, and the players take great pains. They have lovely voices, and we like that they shall develop those voices as much as possible, and that beautiful speech that they are renowned for.

'We always had some ambitions, we always hoped to come to America from the first day, because America is a sort of Mecca for the Irish, when all is said and done. And I am delighted with it.'

The reporter asked if the new literary instinct in Ireland were turning to other channels as well as to the drama.

'I think,' she answered, 'the living young writers are turning to dramatic expression. I think it is simply the fact that when the Irish imagination was let loose from politics it happened to take this form.

'The founding of our theatre probably directed it into that channel. For instance, Mr. Robinson[6] saw one of our plays, and could think of nothing else until he had written one.[7] Mr. Murray,[8] a schoolmaster, saw our plays, and the same was true of him. They saw a chance of showing life as they saw it.

'There is a play we are going to put on week after next—*Mixed Marriage*,[9] dealing with the marriage of Catholics and Protestants—by the son of a pious workingman. In spite of its name it hasn't aroused any antagonism in Ireland. A good many people came on account of its name, thinking there would be a row, but they were disappointed.

'Think of an imaginative mind seeking some way to express itself, and then of the erection of a theatre to give it the opportunity. It is not wonderful that the Irish imagination has turned in that direction. Great numbers of plays are sent us, and if we see the least sign of talent or skill, Mr. Yeats and I write to the authors making suggestions and giving advice. We have never, I think, omitted to write to or see any author that was promising.

'So it has been, you may say, the training of a school of drama.

'Mr. Boyle,[10] whose play[11] we are putting on next week, had been writing stories until he saw our plays, and then he took to drama. In short, they saw the machinery ready and went to it.

'I don't think Ireland has ever had a genius for the novel. Of course, there were plenty of Irish novels, but I don't think that was ever the natural means of expression for the Irish.

'What makes Ireland inclined toward the drama is that it's a great country for conversation. Oscar Wilde said: "We are the best talkers since the Greeks." George Bernard Shaw is a very brilliant talker, so

is Mr. Yeats, and Dr. Mahaffy[12] has written a book[13] on conversation.
'Have you ever listened to Irish servants talking?' asked Lady
Gregory, with one of her infectious smiles. 'They never cease; I have
often envied them their gift of conversation. Take a house in Ireland
at the end of a rainy week; the supply of conversation is quite
inexhaustible, though nothing has happened. And, of course, drama
is conversation arranged.'

She was asked if she meant that there had been no first-class Irish
literature during the century when Irishmen were given up to
politics.

'It was rather dead,' she said, smiling. 'It was an artificial literature
we had in that nineteenth century. Look at the novels that were
brought out of Ireland—Miss Edgeworth,[14] Lever,[15] Lover[16] and the
rest. Some of them I admire very much—Miss Edgeworth's, for
example, but in the main they gave us only a bird's-eye view.'

As the reporter rose to go he heard the audience outside
applauding enthusiastically one of the speeches in *The Playboy of the
Western World.* There wasn't so much as a hiss. He commented on it.

'Yes,' said Lady Gregory, dispassionately, 'but after all it doesn't
make so much difference to us what they do. The question has been
settled. In the universities they are giving these plays to the students
to read. It is not for us to argue now. Synge has won his recognition,
and we are out of the argument. The matter has become one
between the mob, the management and the audience. 'So,' she
added, brightly, 'those are the people to interview. See the Lieblers[17]
and the Police Commissioner.'

NOTES

1. *The Shewing-Up of Blanco Posnet,* by Bernard Shaw, was first performed at the
Abbey Theatre on 25 August 1909. This one-act 'religious tract in dramatic form' was
censored because its references to the Almighty were considered to be blasphemous.

2. *The Bending of the Bough,* by George Moore, opened by the Irish Literary Theatre at
the Gaiety Theatre on 20 February 1900.

3. *The Heather Field,* by Edward Martyn, was first presented by the Irish Literary
Theatre at the Antient Concert Rooms on 9 May 1899.

4. In the autumn of 1897 Synge's hair suddenly began to fall out, and a large lump
formed on the side of his neck. His doctor prescribed ointments for his scalp and
surgery for the 'enlarged gland', as it was described. It was the first manifestation of
Hodgkins Disease, or lymphatic sarcoma, which was to kill him. On 11 December he
was operated on. A second operation was performed in 1907. During that year, Synge
also suffered the first indications of a tumour in his side. In 1908 exploratory surgery
revealed that the growth was inoperable. In early 1909 he entered the Elpis Nursing
Home, where he died soon after, on 24 March 1909.

5. Synge, who was born on 16 April 1871, was almost 38 years old when he died, not
35 as lady Gregory says.

6. Lennox Robinson (1886–1958), playwright and theatrical producer associated
with the Abbey Theatre; a leading figure in the later stages of the Irish literary
renaissance. His plays are remarkable for their stagecraft and lively dialogue. During

1910–14 he was manager of the Abbey Theatre and again from 1919 to 1923, in which year he became a director. He accompanied the Abbey players on several of their tours in the United States and lectured there on the drama during 1928–30. His autobiography, *Curtain Up,* appeared in 1942. See Michael J. O'Neill, *Lennox Robinson* (New York: Twayne Publishers, 1964).

7. *The Clancy Name,* by Lennox Robinson, was first produced at the Abbey Theatre on 8 October 1908.

8. Thomas C. Murray (1873–1959), Irish dramatist whose subjects were drawn from the peasant and farming life of this native county of Cork and were distinguished for sympathetic perception of the deeply religious and sometimes actually mystical quality in the minds of those peasants. He made his name in *Birthright,* produced at the Abbey Theatre in 1910. His plays include *Maurice Harte* (1912), *Spring* (1918), *Aftermath* (1922) and *Autumn Fire* (1924).

9. The first night of *Mixed Marriage,* by St John Ervine, was at the Abbey Theatre on 30 March 1911.

10. William Boyle (1853–1923), Irish dramatist who helped to establish the new type of 'realistic' Irish play which was soon to alter the character of the theatre as Yeats and Lady Gregory had originally conceived it. His plays include *The Building Fund* (1905), *The Eloquent Dempsey* (1906), and *The Mineral Workers* (1906).

11. The first performance of *The Building Fund* was at the Abbey Theatre on 25 April 1905.

12. John Pentland Mahaffy (1839–1919), Provost of Trinity College Dublin. See W.B. Stanford and R.B. McDowell, *Mahaffy; A Biography of an Anglo-Irishman* (London: Routledge, 1972).

13. *The Principles of the Art of Conversation* (London: Macmillan, 1887).

14. Maria Edgeworth (1767–1849), whose *Castle Rackrent* (1800), the first regional novel in English, set Sir Walter Scott on his way.

15. Charles James Lever (1806–72), editor and writer whose novels, set in post-Napoleonic Ireland and Europe, frequently featured lively picaresque heroes. His novels include *Charles O'Malley* (1941) and *Tom Burke of Ours* (1844).

16. Samuel Lover (1797–1868), author of *Legends and Stories of Ireland* (1831) and *Handy Andy* (1842).

17. The American theatrical agents.

Lady Gregory Doesn't Mind the Fighting Evenings*

The scrambled egg evenings at the Maxine Elliott Theatre do not bother Lady Gregory in the least. As she says, 'I am of a fighting race,' and later adds that she is 'quite Irish,' never having left her native soil until she was nearly 19 and when married going to live seven miles from her girlhood home.

Lady Gregory admits grey hair and the fact that she is a

The Sun (New York), (10 Dec 1911)

grandmother, the latter fact softened by the fact that she is a very new one, this milestone in her career having been passed only a week before her departure to the New World.

It is her first trip across the ocean, but she expects to make many more, as the reception accorded her and her company of Irish players, she thinks, seems to warrant this prediction. So little did the stormy voyage harass her that she wrote a play coming over and corrected proofsheets of a new book, besides outlining scenarios &c.

Lady Gregory's hair is parted and waved, fastened in the nape of her neck in a Grecian knot. Over this she wears a black lace scarf which falls low in the back over a simple black gown. This is the costume in which she has already become familiar to theatregoers, whether she is standing in the wings looking on at a specially vital scene, in the chintz hung salon of the theatre, as hostess in a box entertaining celebrities, going and coming from the stage door in the energetic fashion that never destroys her serenity.

She has been interviewed since her arrival and reinterviewed. She adapts herself with grace and ease to the process. 'There was only one misconstruction,' she says smilingly, 'which I had to correct. As a general thing the interviewers have been kind and veracious. But my little company of players do object to being called peasants, perhaps for the reason that they are not peasants, and the morning after our first appearance when the newspapers spoke of them as such I explained to them at rehearsal that I had been equally misrepresented; that they had referred to my blue eyes and to my granddaughter as "he."'

In regard to the fighting scenes that lent additional colour to the first evenings of Synge's *The Playboy of the Western World* Lady Gregory admits that so often has rioting disturbed the stormy tenor of the Irish Players' way that it has now become part of the mosaic of their dramatic life. 'I can't say anything more illuminating on this subject than W.B. Yeats just after his appeal for an endowment for the Irish Theatre:

' "In England the artist has to fight with apathy but in Ireland his enemies are mistaken enthusiasms, old ideals that have outlived their use and the violent prejudices that must exist in every country where the mass of the people have no half interests. Everything becomes vital when it comes to Ireland. It takes to itself wings or claws. Passionate opposition is inspiring but it makes financial independence essential."

'Those are my ideas exactly!'

Lady Gregory makes a verbal departure for a moment, saying that she believes the time is not far distant when people will have on their note paper and business cards 'Telephone Hours So and So,' and it will be understood that the dominating wire can rule only during these intervals. Her need of this has been particularly acute recently, owing to the many calls from friends, acquaintances and even strangers requesting to know if she is 'all right,' if she has been unduly frightened and what she thinks of the *Playboy* disturbances.

'My only disquietude was not at the riot itself but at what it signified; that my people had not freed themselves entirely from the yoke of those traditions which seem so incompatible with your broad, free life here. But I may be doing a great injustice to think even that "my people" have been in any way at fault in this matter. One firecracker under a tin pan can create a terrible din, and one drunken or disorderly person in a crowded gallery is equally disturbing to the general peace.

'The first real riot, which we passed through quite unscathed, not even our feelings lacerated, occurred at the Antient concert rooms in Dublin in 1899, where the Irish Players made their first real essay. This opposition was made to Mr. Yeats's play *Countess Cathleen*. One of his admirers, Horatio Krans, wrote of it that "no drama had ever before been presented in Ireland so inspired with the spirit of the race and so subtly and beautifully steeped in national dyes." The scene of *Countess Cathleen* is laid in old Ireland. She is the great lady of the district, fighting with the conditions of plague, poverty and of demoniac powers which finally, to thwart her good intentions, strip her of her wealth. She at length sells her soul to these demons for gold to relieve her beloved people, but a vision at the end of the play tells that she is forgiven because God judges the intention, not the deed.

'Some rough and ready theologians saw fit to object to the suggestion that God had forgiven a woman who so far forgot her duty, intimating it as a reflection upon the doctrines of Catholic orthodoxy. Their banding together to break up the performances, interfered with by the police who acted in the interests of law and order, really made thinking people wonder what time of day it is with certain people in Ireland.

'Several other battles have marked our steady ongoing, the most severe that which raged about the production of Bernard Shaw's *Blanco Posnet,* which had been refused by the censor. We believed this act to be purely hypocritical and stood firmly by our intention.[1] It required courage to do that, because we were threatened by the officers of the Crown with the loss of our patent and a fine so heavy that it would eat up all profits. We put the play on at the Abbey, billing it for the week of the Horse Show. We had committee meetings up to the last rehearsal debating whether we should fly in the face of this powerful opposition, but the Irish blood was up and we stood by our guns manfully. Heaven is on the side of the strongest battalions, said Napoleon; our battalions were strong in conviction if not in numbers, and we won out triumphantly. The theatre was crowded every night and *Blanco Posnet* was one of our big successes.

'You can understand how tremendous the feeling in Ireland has been over these plays by this incident. There is a certain public house in a certain back street in Dublin where a few months after the trouble over *The Playboy* the owner's wife for some reason or other, possibly a sudden fit of housewifely industry, ordered one of her potboys to take our bills of that drāma out of the window. He said "If they go, I go." A second potboy was called and to the request he made the same answer. Finally the owner came downstairs and shouted "Leave the damn things where they are." They stayed.'

It is with great difficulty that Lady Gregory can be induced to leave the interesting topic of the achievements of those who have been associated with the success of the National Theatre, Yeats, Synge, Douglas Hyde and others, and tell something about her own personal work.

'There are many moments when I feel as if I shall have to leave all this theatrical work, the writing of scenarios, for others, the time killing processes of organization, stage managing, rehearsing, to devote myself entirely to the study, collecting, translating and the purely literary functions of the Gaelic work. There are such stores of material yet untouched, such wonderful volumes written only in the memories of the old who are fast passing on, leaving nothing tangible behind them, such marvellous possibilities, and the day is so short, its demands so insistent. One cannot do everything!'

'I made three attempts to learn Gaelic. The laughter of a large family, the cruel blast that has destroyed so many tender flowers, prevented the first from fruition. After my early marriage I made a second trial, choosing for school teacher an old laborer, but my innocent ambition was misconstrued. Ireland was at that time a hotbed of suspicion. What did such an unprecedented act imply? For the sake of peace I dropped my primer efforts and it was not until Ireland was torn apart following the Parnell imbroglio, when all tables of value were changed, that the old idea was resurrected and this time I studied and learned unmolested.

'It is not an easy language to learn; it is unbelievably difficult. Rules of grammar and construction have had to be made to suit a language which went merrily on during its formative time without regard to set forms. Consonants have been dropped at will so as to make the rhythm more perfect, and in consequence the written and the spoken words are so strangely different that you doubt their relationship all the time. The taking away of the consonants left nothing to hang your hat on.

'I was the first to write in the Irish dialect—that is, the English of Gaelic thinking people. I wrote in it before Synge did. He said he was amazed to find in my *Cuchulain of Muirthemne* his desired dialect.

Several of my plays, published in book form,[2] are in the repertory of the National Theatre. *Twenty-Five,* my first, has had a checkered career, suppressed because it was too sensational. I am rewriting *The Workhouse Ward.* I believe in rewriting and bringing out again plays that have had changes made in them to suit the dramatic demand which a literary production does not always meet. Intention and desire come, you press your idea, then comes the iron hand of technique forcing that expression into the mould of convention. The play I wrote on the steamer is to be published in the *Outlook,* and I have with me a short, unpublished play which is to come out before long.

'The original incorporators of the Irish National Theatre Society have never been paid for their services, as such. By our new contract we cannot, if we would. We have only the small royalties that come when any of our plays are produced, but the criticism that has been made that we are not seeking new material is unfounded. We read and search anxiously in the mass of manuscript that comes in, much of it available for other theatres than ours which have not a distinct purpose to fulfil.

'Those who have answered successfully these requirements, besides some already mentioned, are T.C. Murray, who wrote *The Village Schoolmaster;* Mr Irvine, son of a Belfast workingman; Mr Robinson, a Cork Man; Miss Alice Milligan, who wrote *The Last Feast of the Fianna. The Bending of the Bough,* by George Moore, was very popular, as was *Maeve,* by Mr Martyn. The first Gaelic play written as such was given at a Dublin theatre when we produced *The Twisting of the Rope,* by Douglas Hyde. This was an adaptation made in three or four days by him at my home at Coole from one of the Hanrahan stories of Mr. Yeats. *Dearmuid and Grania* was a heroic play that Yeats and Moore wrote in collaboration. This was produced under the temporary chaperonage of F.R. Benson, the Shakespearian manager who relieved us of our onerous duties for a time.

'Briefly, many of the requirements of these plays may be summed up in the statement that they must present Ireland past and present to the sympathy of the world and throw a light on all the phases of Irish character, not entirely cutting off those with which we are so familiar on the stage, but adding to them, interpreting them anew.

'I have been asked why we do not present these plays as curtain raisers. To do that would defeat the whole object of our plan. Charles Frohman[3] saw that when a few years ago he brought over the clever Fays, connected in the beginning of our work with us at the Abbey Theatre. He gave these plays by themselves, thus preserving the atmosphere, and while they did not make a great success they no doubt helped to pave the way for this, the second appearance of the Irish Players.

'The failure then to make a big success may have been due to the fact that they were given in a large theatre. In the beginning of our productions Mr. Yeats objected strongly, as did I, to the stagy methods of the London actors, and it was not until we had advanced far enough along to have our own people interpret them that we were satisfied. Our people do not seem to play to the audience, but the audience seems to be looking on at the unfolding of the scenes. A small theatre helps this illusion.

'When I saw the Sicilian players I was immensely impressed with one salient point, the perfection of gesture. Gesture to the Latin race is as natural as breathing. Our people do not gesture and to try to make them would be foolish.

'The material we have is the voice. The Irish people have beautiful, rhythmic voices, and we have made these our component of value. Since we have been here I have had many conversations and received many letters commenting on this fact.

'All through the country I have found a new interest in the Gaelic movement. Prof. Baker[4] of Harvard has done much to further our work. I lectured at Smith, Wellesley, Yale and other educational centres. In every place I was surprised and pleased at the attention and information I found. In Boston many of the tenants on our estate in Ireland, emigrants to the New World, came to the theatre and then to visit me. With several of them I took tea. I find them often homesick, but I have noticed that when they come back it is usually for a visit. The old homes, transfigured by their vivid imaginations, seem woefully small and uninviting. Once a strange woman came to our place at Coole and asked to see my husband. When she had an interview she put some money in his hand, about $20 as I remember, and then went away. We never knew who she was; apparently some one executing a dying request, which may have meant the return of a "conscience" fund. She said that she had come from America to do this and was going right back again. She looked out of the window and commented on the disappointment it had been to her to see the places she had left as a child. That was the only clue we had to her mysterious coming and we never found out anything else, but there is an Irish play in that incident.

'Your own country was the first to help the Irish Theatre. Our first £50 was the gift of John Quinn, a well known lawyer of New York city, who has always been interested in the Gaelic movement, is a friend of Douglas Hyde and of Mr. Yeats, and sent in answer to our first request for funds to carry on the work of protest against the current belief that Ireland is the home of buffoonery. We have since then bought the Abbey Theatre and have a large part of the £5,000 contributed, which seems necessary to carry on the enlarged work which commenced in concert hall rooms and which has now its season every year in London at the Court Theatre, Sloane Square, and will apparently have an American season as well. That is not doing so badly in thirteen years, is it? It was through the influence displayed by Miss Horniman, who became interested in our London work, that we went into the Abbey Theatre of Dublin, reconstructed and given rent-free, with the addition of a subsidy which expired in 1910.'

Lady Gregory places no time limit on the duration of the American tour. 'I came over at a week's notice,' she says, 'and just as long as the interest of the public holds out we shall remain. At present the Abbey Theatre is tenanted by a class of sixty under Norman Muncke and from these pupils we shall draw for a second company, so that when we come again our own playhouse will not have to closed, as happened this time.'

NOTES

1. Lady Gregory, as patentee of the Abbey Theatre, was threatened with loss of its patent if she allowed production of the play as it stood. She called on an official at the Dublin Castle, who asked that the 'blasphemous' expressions be deleted; she refused, explaining that the blasphemer's defiance of heaven constituted the subject of the play. Bernard Shaw was enchanted, and he rewarded Lady Gregory by an affection that was to last to the end of her life.

2. Lady Gregory, *Seven Short Plays* (Dublin: Maunsel, 1909).

3. Charles Frohman (1860–1915), American theatrical manager who was a leading figure in the group of theatrical managers know as Theatrical Syndicate.

4. Professor George Pierce Baker (1866–1935), who made his reputation as teacher of dramatic composition in his course in playwriting; author of *Dramatic Technique* (Boston: Houghton Mifflin, 1909).

Lady Gregory: Guiding Genius of the Irish Players*

CHAUNCEY L. PARSONS

Every patron of Maxine Elliott's Theatre during the stay of the Irish Players must have become familiar with a figure in a trailing black gown, with a black lace mantilla over her grey hair, for such a person hovered about the house like a sort of patron saint. It was Lady Augusta Gregory, of course, as you might have been informed a hundred times an evening, had you cared to listen to the

*New York Dramatic Mirror, LXVI (27 Dec 1911) 5.

explanations of those that knew. She was present at every performance of her company—or nearly every performance—absenting herself only to watch George Arliss[1] and Niagara Falls, and possibly one or two other wonders on exhibition in this country. When it comes to the Irish Players, she does not believe in the ancient maxim that a watched pot never boils, but she puts to practical test the other old saw about eternal vigilance and the price of success. In this case, the event has justified the method.

Particularly selecting a straight-backed chair in the green room of the theatre, Lady Gregory sat with folded hands, the very picture of contentment and affability. Her expression and manner invited easy confidence.

'So much has been said about the past history of the company,' said Lady Gregory, 'that I'd prefer to talk about the future now. With the continued success of the movement, it is highly probable that a school of acting will be established at the Abbey Theatre in Dublin, or in connection with it, and that we shall organize more than one company from the material thus cultivated. We really need one company in Dublin all the time, and could very easily send others through England, America, and possibly Australia. In view of the lively interest that has surrounded us wherever we have journeyed. I am sure of the feasibility of such an extension. Now that the hardest part of the matter is at an end—the obtaining of a foothold—the rest should follow with comparative ease, if we continue to exercise care throughout our labour.'

Beyond a doubt, Lady Gregory's rosy plans for the future gain substantial probability by what has already been accomplished. Moreover, the Irish Players in New York have steadily grown in popularity among the more intelligent and orderly class of theatregoers. Although received at first rather coolly by the critics, they have gradually won over nearly all of the hard-shelled dramatic journalists, and are certainly condemned by none.

'Had I not become interested in the Gaelic movement,' said Lady Gregory, 'I should doubtless have turned my attention to the music halls of England,' She is essentially a woman of the theatre, as she herself declares. Perhaps no other field for endeavor has ever seriously presented itself to her mind. 'The music halls appeal to me because they reach such an enormous audience—all of the poorer members of society who are financially unable to Patronize the first-class theatres. I have, for instance, seen the Tivoli Music Hall in London crowded with spectators who paid perhaps sixpence apiece for admission. See what a tremendous range that gives anybody who succeeds in pleasing their fancy.

'From the whole programme that I have in mind—the one at the Tivoli—there were two numbers which one would call vulgar. All the rest were quite harmless, and yet were just as popular. The masses, as we are pleased to term the poorer people, don't want vulgarity, just because it is vulgarity. Like the rest of us, they want to be entertained, and they are just as willing to be entertained decently as anybody else.

'Last summer, one or two of my own pieces were done in music halls, with results quite equal to my hopes. *The Workhouse Ward* was received very cordially, and most people agree that the comedy isn't vulgar.' Lady Gregory smiled gently. 'That little experience has confirmed my earlier opinion in the practicability of working in vaudeville.

'I believe in beginning at the bottom to build up the drama, you see. It is much like erecting a house. The Chinese are the only ones who begin with the roof and work down to the ground.' Even if Lady Gregory had noticed the similar method adopted by American contractors in constructing skyscrapers, she probably would not admit that even in the land where skyscrapers were invented, the paradoxical method could be satisfactorily applied to dramatic art.

Many people have argued that the first-class theatres set the tone for theatrical productions, which gradually permeates the rest of the stage; many others have argued that progress must start in the houses of second-class, which attract so many more patrons. The truth of the matter is that any new idea has to struggle for years with determination before it gains momentum enough to be felt, as an appreciable force in the strong current of tradition. Reformers with the best of intentions are objects of suspicion, because society has a tremendous fear either of leaping from the frying pan into the fire, or else of making itself ridiculous by chasing after false gods. Since old conventions are continually getting sluggish and muddy, however, we sorely need the reformers to break through old banks with a new impetus that clears the steam. Let them begin in the music halls or the theatres, they are equally welcome.

'My energies are so taken up by the Irish Players that I shall not attempt the music hall movement,' continued Lady Gregory. 'One thing at a time, you know.' Then, with the utmost placidity, she added, 'As I grow old, I find it advisable to narrow the banks, as one of my friends says.' A mere spectator is forced to observe that the narrowing is not visible from the outside.

'My time has been so occupied by the business of this trip that I haven't had an opportunity to see much of the American stage. I went to see Disraeli[2] a few nights ago, and it struck me as a most remarkable performance, but rather ghastly because I knew Disraeli. Shortly after my marriage, I attended a function at which he was present, and although he was suddenly called away just as I was about to be presented to him, I recall very clearly his stooping figure in the black velvet coat and the diamond star. So, when I sawl Mr Arliss in the play, it gave me an uncanny feeling.

'The characterization, however, is very true, because Disraeli was always so ready to concern himself in the little human details of life, even when burdened by the cares of state. For that reason, the pretty love affair does not seem out of place, or forced in for purely theatrical reasons.

'The production, as a piece of stage craft, impressed me most favourably, because it is all so quiet. English plays are apt to be so fidgety that they make me feel restless and uncomfortable, but in this drama of Mr Parker's everything moves smoothly and tastefully to the conclusion. It is a mercy the telephone had not been invented in Disraeli's day, for if it had been, he would have been chattering to it at every other breath.' This remark illuminates the general spirit of the acting of the Irish Players, which is all remarkably simple. Against such a Doric background, every gesture has its value. As long as simplicity does not descent into stiffness, it is an entirely admirable theory and has really been the working principle of every great artist. In this matter, however, as in every other lofty point, one step will carry the actor from the sublime to the ridiculous.

'I can't be away from the theatre when new plays are on,' said Lady Gregory as the sound of laughter penetrated from the front of the house. 'I must see not only how the play succeeds, but also how the audience succeeds. That is even more important. Audiences change nightly, so it is a new play to me every time I attend the performance. The company remembers the audiences, too.' Lady Gregory smiled significantly. 'I believe the record is held by an audience in some provincial English town, which never laughed once through an entire performance of *Spreading the News*. I don't recall the place, but ask the cast and they could tell you.' Doubtless the cast have laughed enough since to make up for the deficiency.

'Somebody once remarked to Toole[3] the actor, "I should think you'd get tired of acting the same part over and over again." Toole replied, "I should think you'd get tired of telling the same old stories over and over again." Roles and stories age, but audiences never. The public keeps a play young.

'American audiences have been pretty kind to us, even when we were doing *Blanco Posnet*. We were sure of our Irish plays, but we didn't know what Americans might think of a Colorado hero.[4] Mr Shaw himself, however, was much pleased by our production, so we ventured to try it. A more fantastically and delightfully impossible play, even the Irish company hardly possesses, and Mr. Shaw will have to try harder than that to make us say such unkind things about him as he has said about America.'

Lady Gregory, however, took up the cudgels in defence of her friend. 'Mr Shaw is not really so black as he has been painted. He once told me that some nuns were advertising for a watch dog which should be wildly ferocious at some hours and perfectly meek at others, and he thought himself well qualified for the position. When Mr Shaw's remarks are circulated, it is much like the game of Russian Scandal. Number one whispers a sentence to number two, who repeats it to number three in the same fashion, and so on around the room. The final form usually hasn't an atom of relationship to the innocent sentence that started.

'By this same law, I suppose that London thinks the première of *The Playboy* in New York was a repitition of the Boston Massacre. I spent the time kneeling in the wings telling them to go on with the play, but to save their voices, because they'd have to do it over. As I wasn't hit, I can't complain: only I hope they will boil the potatoes next time.' Lady Gregory laughed at the recollection of the event, therby finally proving her great good sense.

'In Boston, I was pleased to find that the public was already familiar with the plays in our repertoire. Professor Baker, of Harvard, had done much to rouse interest. People used to come to me and ask why various lines and scenes had been changed. One has a mental image of Boston studiously keeping tabs on the actors by means of texts of the play in their hands, perhaps murmuring inwardly because the insufficient light during *The Rising of the Moon* deprives them of this diversion. It is not a bad method, either, if one wants to get the most out of a play.

'Our American engagement has been extended till the end of February, but then we must return to Dublin. We must not stay long enough to get the American accent, for that would destroy our *raison d'être,* and we should be disowned in Ireland. Already, however, the members of the company have individually roused the interest of the public. Spectators no longer turn to their programmes to find out who has just entered the scene. The audiences know the actors and like to see them do various parts. It is a business asset as well as an excellent training for the actors, who gain flexibility by the different requirements of different roles. That is the way we grow.'

With this optimistic explanation of the past and forecast of the future, Lady Gregory led the way back to the front of the house, from which it was apparent she had been kept quite as long as she could endure.

NOTES

1. George Arliss (1868–1946), an English actor; played leading roles in both England and the United States. He appeared on the screen in the days of the silent films and later in sound films. His autobiography, *Up the Years from Bloomsbury,* appeared in 1927.

2. *Disraeli,* a play in four acts by Louis Napolean Parker, was published and produced in 1911. Set in England in the early 1870s, it was presented as a portrayal of 'some of the racial, social, and political prejudices Disraeli fought against and conquered'. The play was an immensely popular vehicle for George Arliss.

3. John Lawrence Toole (1830–1906), the English comedian.

4. The play is the account of the conversion of a blackguard in the Wild West of America.

Irish Play Moral*

While Mayor Harrison conferred yesterday with Corporation Counsel Sexton as to whether or not the city has power to prohibit 'The Playboy of the Western World' from being staged in Chicago, Lady Augusta Gregory sat calmly in her apartments at the Hotel La Salle and upheld the moral status of the production.

She declared that there is nothing in the play that could harm man, woman or child, and further stated that she was at a loss to understand why 'The Playboy' has caused such a storm of protest among the Irish people wherever it has been staged.

One of the principal objections to the production is a part contained in one of the acts where an Irish countryman slays his father and is praised by his friends for the deed. Irish descendants claim that the play is not true to life.

SAYS PLAY IS NOT TRUE TO LIFE

'Of course "The Playboy" is not true to life' declared Lady Gregory yesterday. 'No play is exactly true to life, or it would never achieve success. Shakespeare's plays are not true to life and they are not being criticised. The question of the morality of the play may be left safely to the authorities that pass upon it and to the people who come to see it, and so far that has been done triumphantly wherever we have been.'

The corporation counsel's opinion will be returned to Mayor Harrison today and if the opinion states that the mayor has power to prohibit the production, that action will probably be taken.

'Unless the corporation counsel finds a legal objection, I have nothing to do but obey the order of the city council, which body has declared itself against the play,' said Mayor Harrison last night.

SAYS MAYOR CANNOT STOP PERFORMANCE

Attorney Charles G. Hamill, who has been engaged by Lady Gregory,

Inter Ocean (Chicago) (31 Jan 1912) 7.

declared, however, that he does not expect any legal move will be necessary. He is confident that Mayor Harrison will be advised that he has no power to prevent the play.

Copies of the play are on the way here from Terre Haute, Ind., where the company appears tonight, and these will be submitted to the mayor and corporation counsel today. The players are all Irish by birth and had never left Ireland until they came to England on the present tour.

Lady Gregory smiled when told that one of the men's names who objected to the play was Alderman McInerney.

'That's a strange coincidence,' declared Lady Gregory. 'In one[1] of our plays the principal character is a good old Irishman by the name of Mike McInernes.

NOTE

1. *The Workhouse Ward.*

Our Trials and Triumphs*

LADY GREGORY

It is hard to say what my object was in first taking up the idea of a native theater for native plays of the Irish. Probably my first idea was to make an opportunity for the production of the plays of William Butler Yeats, who helped to found the theater and who has provided the Abbey company with its most effective poetical plays. In the beginning, with crude scenery and little money, we started with English players but as the movement grew we hit upon the happy thought of employing only Irish actors, many of whom were peasants. In fact, we became a national institution almost by accident.

Many of our plays at first aroused much criticism, and we were attacked by both the government and the church. Now, however, the residents of Dublin and its vicinity regard us as a possession of the city. One of our plays, 'The Playboy of the Western World,' a satire by Synge, seemed especially offensive for a time. When it was first put on there was almost a riot. Another, Bernard Shaw's 'The Showing

*Extracted from 'The Story of the Irish Players,' *Sunday Record-Herald* (Chicago) (4 Feb 1912).

Up of Blanco Posnet,' which was written especially for us, was censored in London. We took it to Dublin, and although the viceroy used every influence, political, religious and popular, to prevent our producing it, we did produce it.

We do not profess that all the plays we give can please everybody. The Irish proverb says, 'If you wish to grow old you must eat hot and cold,' and so a theater that had stuck to providing for any one class of people would have died long ago. Unionists have objected to my plays, 'The Rising of the Moon,'[1] 'The Gaol Gate,'[2] and to Mr Yeats' 'Cathleen-ni-Houlihan'.[3] Only 'The Playboy' aroused serious general opposition.

DUBLIN WANTS THEM BACK

But even in the case of that play we were by no means 'hissed out of Dublin'; on the contrary, our players had a tremendous reception on their last appearance on the stage before they sailed and a great sending off at the station. Dublin is very proud of them and proud of knowing we have had such a success in America.

The only grumble I have heard from Dublin for a long time is that we are staying away these winter months. We have been much pressed to stay all through the winter because of our success in Boston and elsewhere.

Our players are, without exception, Catholics, and are held in the highest esteem not only in Ireland, their native place, but in London, Oxford, Cambridge, Manchester and, indeed, wherever they have played. The extraordinary purity and delicacy of their acting are especially appreciated. No one who knows them personally or who has seen their work could for a moment think of associating them with anything of an indecent or immoral tendency.

Archbishop Healey of our own diocese in Dublin and Mgr Lahey, the parish priest, are most friendly to us. I think our critics have been misinformed. If they saw the plays they would think differently about them.

It is true some of our plays are a little harsh, but then our younger dramatists are realistic, and they show Ireland as they see it through their own temperaments.

THE DIGNITY OF IRELAND

We believe we have elevated the dignity of Ireland. We have shown the world, who knew it not, that the old culture of Ireland had not died, but was still with us.

Some have said we hurt the cause of Irish home rule. On the contrary, we have helped it. In England we were asked to put on one of Synge's plays—'The Tinker's Wedding'[4]—but we refused because it hurt the feelings of Catholics.

We believe and know that our theater, taken as a whole, has added to the dignity of Ireland. It is watched with the greatest interest and appreciation on the continent of Europe; Australia and South Africa are trying to found repertory theaters on its model, and the desire to do so is being very widely expressed in America in intellectual centers and educational institutions especially.

A question I am often asked is, 'Why do you come to America?' In reply I can say only that our grandfather's chief ambition was to make what they called the 'grand tour' through France, Spain and Italy. Nowadays every Irishman hopes to see America, because so many of his friends and relatives have come here. Then I imagine we wanted to come to show you what we could do in our little home theater with Irish stock.

NOTES

1. *The Rising of the Moon* had its première at the Abbey Theatre on 9 March 1907. The play opens with a police sergeant on guard near a quay. Alarm is out for an escaped Fenian patriot. A ballad singer engages the sergeant in conversation, which drifts toward the past. The sergeant ponders the fate that made him a policeman instead of a patriot rebel; he joins the ballad singer in old patriotic songs. As the ballad singer chants, a boat approaches; and the sergeant realises that his companion is the escaped prisoner. Restraining himself, he lets the patriot go away; then, thinking of the £100 reward, he says, 'I wonder if I'm as big a fool as I think I am!'

2. *The Gaol Gate* was first performed at the Abbey Theatre on 20 October 1906. The play is a tragedy with a strong nationalist tone.

3. *Cathleen ni Houlihan* opened at St Teresa's Hall, Dublin, on 2 April 1902. Peter Gillane and his family are getting ready for the marriage of his son, Michael, when an old woman comes in. It is Cathleen, the daughter of Houlihan (the personification of Ireland). She talks of the beautiful fields she has lost to strangers, and of the men who died for her. Her stirring words and songs inspire Michael to forget his bride and follow Cathleen. W.B. Yeats spent sleepless nights wondering about the effects of the play's patriotic exhortations:

> Did that play of mine send out
> Certain men the English shot?

4. When Elkin Mathews, the publisher, asked Synge about *The Tinker's Wedding* Synge told him that it was 'likely to displease a good many of our Dublin friends'. One of the early decisions of the Irish National Theatre Society was not to produce *The Tinker's Wedding*. The play was eventually published in 1908.

Lady Gregory Counselled us Wisely*

MAURICE BROWNE

The Irish Players were about to visit Chicago. Cathleen Nesbitt, whom I had known since she was a schoolgirl, wrote of riots in Boston over *The Playboy:* Chicago, that notorious city, might be even worse; would my fiancée and I—she had heard that I was engaged: her sympathies to the wretched girl—patrol the first performance? We would, hawk-eyed; was not Synge the greatest dramatist since Shakespeare? On the opening night there were hardly a hundred people present, most of them our sentries. There was no disturbance. Disappointing.

Thereafter throughout the Irish Players' stay we forgathered with them daylong and nightlong. In those years the Company had no equal on the English-speaking stage for either team-work or individual performance. Sara Allgood[1] at her prime was, with the possible exceptions in years to come of Beulah Bondi and Nellie Van, the finest character-actress whom I have seen; I have watched her play four old Irishwomen in four one-act plays on the same night and, beyond the facts that all were Irish, female and old, they did not have a common characteristic. In *Cathleen ni Houlihan* she stood, a withered crone, against an open doorway and grew before my eyes from five-foot-nothing till her head touched the stars. When I asked how she did it, she answered: 'Sure, I don't know; I suppose I just think of God and Ireland.' We asked where she and her fellow-players had learned that deep and purposeful repose which was their hallmark. 'Sure,' she said, 'when we started we didn't know enough to move, so we stood still; now we know better than to move unless we must.'

Meanwhile Lady Gregory counselled us wisely and with razor tongue: 'By all means start your own theatre; but make it in your own image. Don't engage professional players; they have been spoiled for your purpose. Engage and train, as we of the Abbey have

*Extracted from *Too Late to Lament; An Autobiography* (London: Gollancz, 1955; Bloomington, Indiana: Indiana University Press, 1956) pp. 115–17.

done, amateurs: shopgirls, school-teachers, counter-jumpers; cut-throat-thieves rather than professionals. And prepare to have your hearts broken.'

She told us a tale from Plutarch. I have forgotten its hero's name: Agathon will serve. Agathon was a famous actor; he was also a fine actor. One day in a fit of anger he struck his son; the boy, stepping backward from the blow, stumbled, fell, struck his head, died. The father, broken by remorse, retired from the stage. But he continued to study the plays of his favourite dramatist, Euripides, particularly *Hippolytus.*

In that play Theseus, king of Trozen, has recently married a young wife, Phaedra; Hippolytus is his son by an earlier marriage. Phaedra falls in love with her stepson and in his father's absence tries to seduce him; the lad indignantly repulses her. When Theseus returns home Phaedra tells him that Hippolytus has tried to rape her; the father, furiously refusing to hear his son's protestations of innocence, banishes him. As Hippolytus leaves the palace, monstrous sea-beasts—unloosed by these storms of lust, lies, rage, revenge—trample the lad underfoot. He is carried back into his father's presence, again protests his innocence and dies. His father realizes, too late, that his son has spoken the truth.

When the time of Agathon's purgation had been fulfilled, he returned to the stage. Henceforth he played one part only, Theseus. Each time that he played it, throughout the play's closing scene he held in his hands, as a chalice, the funeral urn containing the ashes of his own son.

'Yes, yes, yes,' Nellie Van and I exclaimed, 'that is what we mean by theatre; that is the kind of theatre we want. But how can we start any kind of theatre, let alone such a theatre as that? We have no experience, no money, no players, no place to play.'

'We had none of those things either,' Lady Gregory replied. 'It is true that we were not so poor as you; but you have one asset which we lacked: youth. And we had one liability which you will not incur: we confused theatric with literary values. One of you'—she glanced at Nellie Van—'already sees that those values are different; the other'—she glanced at me—'will learn it, slowly and painfully. He will learn that poetry must serve the theatre before it can again rule there.' Then, like my father at the Ipswich swimming-bath, she picked us up and chucked us into the deep end: 'Strike out, my children. And God bless you.'

NOTES

Maurice Browne (1881–1955), dramatist, manager and actor. He was born and educated in England, but first made his name in the United States, where he is credited with the founding of the Little Theatre movement by his establishment in 1912 of the

Chicago Little Theatre, which he directed for several years. After several productions in New York he appeared in London for the first time in 1927, and two years later he produced Sheriff's *Journey's End* at the Savoy Theatre. He was later responsible for the management of the Globe and Queen's Theatres.

1. Sara Allgood (1883–1950), Irish actress, whose early career is bound up with the history of the Abbey Theatre. In 1914 she joined the Liverpool Repertory Theatre company. She made her last appearance on the stage in New York in 1940, and then appeared only in films. The finest performances of her career were Juno Boyle in *Juno and the Paycock* and Bessie Burgess in *The Plough and the Stars*—both plays by Sean O'Casey. Sara Allgood became an intimate friend of Lady Gregory and a frequent visitor to Coole. See Elizabeth Coxhead, 'Sally and Molly,' *Daughters of Erin* (London: Secker & Warburg, 1965) pp. 167–224.

Lady Gregory and the Abbey Theater*

JOHN QUINN

I was away from New York when the Abbey Theater company of Dublin first came here, and I did not see them play until the end of their first week. In writing to a friend to explain who they were and what they had accomplished, I pointed out the perfect naturalness of their acting, the simplicity of their methods, their freedom from all distracting theatricalism and 'stage business,' their little resort to gesture, the beautiful rhythm of their speech, the absence of extensive and elaborate scenery and stage-settings, and the delightful suggestion of spontaneity given by their apparently deliberate throwing away of technical accomplishments in the strict sense of the word. I said that too many theaters have costly scenery and expensive properties to cover the poverty of art in the play or the players, just as poor paintings are sold by dealers in big glaring gold frames; and had the same refined quality, not always apparent at the first glance, that old Chinese paintings are seen to have when placed alongside of modern paintings by Western artists.

As I observed the fine craftsmanship of the actors, without a single false note, each seeming to get into the very skin of the part that he impersonated, my thoughts went back some eight or nine years to what were the beginnings of this whole enterprise.

On a Sunday in August in 1902 I traveled with Jack B. Yeats,[1] the artist, from Dublin, through Mullingar to Athenry, and thence by

Outlook (New York) IC (16 Dec 1911) 916–19.

side-car to Killeeneen, in County Galway. On the way from Athenry to Killeeneen we passed little goups of bright-eyed men and women, always with a heart laugh and a cheery word 'for the American' and 'a pleasant journey to you.' They were on their way to a 'Feis' (or festival) that was to be held that afternoon at Killeeneen, where the blind Connacht poet Raftery was buried. The Feis was held on rising ground in a field beside the road. There were perhaps a hundred side-cars and other vehicles and five or six hundred men and women at the meeting. On a raised platform sat Dr. Douglas Hyde, the President of the Gaelic League; Edward Martyn from Tillyra Castle; Lady Gregory from Coole; and others in charge fo the Feis. W.B. Yeats, the poet, and his brother, Jack B. Yeats, the artist, and myself stood in the crowd and watched the spectacle.

Yeats told me that Lady Gregory had heard some time before that there was in the neighbourhood a book in Irish with songs of Raftery. She had found it in the possession of an old stone-cutter near Killeeneen. She got a loan of the book and gave it to Dr. Hyde, and he discovered in it seventeen of Raftery's songs. Douglas Hyde has since edited and translated a book of the songs and poems of Raftery, and he gives many interesting stories of the bard. He told me that Sunday that it was to the kindness of Lady Gregory that he owed many of his stories of Raftery. She had got, from a man who, when he was a boy, was present at Raftery's death, a full account of it. The poet was buried in the old churchyard of Killeeneen, among the people whom he knew. In August, 1900, there had been a great gathering there. Lady Gregory was the chief organizer of the gathering. She had raised a high stone over Raftery's grave with the name of the poet in Irish upon it. It was she who had thought of doing it, Dr. Hyde told me that Sunday afternoon, and it was upon her that the cost, or most of the cost, had fallen.

Prizes were given at the Feis for Irish singing, for the recitation of old poems, the telling of old stories all in Irish, and for traditional Irish dancing, flute-playing, and Irish music. A little girl from the Claddagh, the fishermen's quarter of Galway, took two or three of the prizes, and a week or ten days after, in going through the Claddagh, I saw her and spoke to her, and she remembered seeing me at the Feis. There was an old man there, and it took much persuasion to get him to mount the platform and tell his story. He hung back diffidently for a long time, but finally a lane was opened in the crowd and he got his courage up and marched bravely to the platform, and, gesticulating with a big blackthorn stick, made a great speech in Irish. Hyde translated parts of it for Yeats and me, and told us how the old man had boasted that he had been at Raftery's dying and had 'held the candle to him.'

Over the platform was a big green banner with letters in Irish on it and a picture of Raftery as an old man remembered him, painted by a sympathetic artist of the neighbourhood. The Feis continued until some time after nightfall. The guests for Lady Gregory's place at Coole, some sixteen miles away, returned on two side-cars: Lady Gregory, W.B. Yeats, and myself on one; Douglas Hyde, Mrs. Hyde, and Jack Yeats on the other.

It was black night when the lights of Coole welcomed us. Lady Gregory got down from the car first, and, turning to me and extending her hand, said, with a pleasant smile, 'Welcome to Coole.' I wish I could picture something of the charm that hangs around Coole, of its tangled woods, its stately trees, the lake, the winding paths, the two beautiful old gardens, and the view of the distant Burren hills. There seemed to be magic in the air, enchantment in the woods and the beauty of the place, and the best talk and stories I ever found anywhere. The great library was to me a delight, and Jack Yeats told me that Lady Gregory had made a catalogue of it herself. She seemed to me to have a strong sense of property, and took great pride in and had done her share in keeping up the fabled 'Seven Woods of Coole,' planting every year trees for the coming generation. And I remembered that Arthur Young in his 'A Tour in Ireland' had referred to a visit that he made over a hundred years before to the Coole of that period, and had found the Gregory of that time walling and 'improving his land with great spirit,' and planting the trees which are now among the glories of the place.

Every summer for some years Yeats had spent several months at Coole. He is the best talker I have ever listened to, and he does love to talk. So long as he can amuse himself and interest others with good talk he will not write. Lady Gregory devoted herself to his work. With infinite tact and sympathy she has got the best out of him, and the world of letters owes it chiefly to her that in the last ten years Yeats has done so much creative work and has been able to devote himself so fully to the Irish theater. At Coole he had leisure and delightful surroundings which in London he could not have. He was able there to dream out and plan out his poems and plays. She threw herself into his plans for work, worked with him, worked from his dictation, copied out his rough drafts, arranged his manuscripts for him, read out to him in the evenings from the great books of the world at times when his eyesight was poor and he could not read at night, and stimulated his genius by her helpful understanding of all his plans and ideas.

One of the chief charms of my repeated visits to Coole lay in the stores of good talk and anecdotes by Yeats and Hyde, who were there at the time of each of my visits, and in my interest in the genius and personality of Yeats and Lady Gregory. During the whole time of our visit the sparkle and brilliancy of the conversation never failed. Lady

Gregory's interest in the people about her was untiring. With a power of work that any man of letters might envy, she had the faculty of laying aside her work and making all her guests enjoy to the full the pleasant side of life and the delights of social intercourse. Her enthusiasm was infectious, and those who came in contact with her—Yeats, Hyde, Synge, and the rest—became or were made her helpers and associates.

But with all Yeats's debt to her, she also owes much to him. He is the most disinterested of writers. I have known him to take infinite pains, make long journeys, and give hours and days of his time to encouraging other writers, starting them on the right way and giving them unfailing help and assistance. He is incapable of praising bad work even though it be by a friend, and incapable of condemning good work even though it be by an enemy. He was Lady Gregory's severest critic, and she owes to him a big debt for encouragement, criticism, and help in the writing of her books and plays, and because he 'taught her her trade.' He is, above all things, the man of letters. His mind is one of the most subtle I have ever known. He delights in discussing art and philosophy, and will talk for hours and hours on politics, diplomacy, and international affairs. I remember how interested he became in a volume of Nietzsche that I had with me, and how in reading out from it he quickly pointed out the resemblance of some of Nietzsche's ideas to Blake.

One morning Lady Gregory, Dr. Hyde, and myself wandered through one of the beautiful old gardens. She named over the names of this, that, and the other flower until Hyde said that if she just wrote down the names there was matter for a sonnet ready for Yeats. Yeats was very happy there, and he had just finished a poem on 'The Seven Woods of Coole,' and he was so pleased with it that he kept murmuring it over and over again, and these lines from it have remained in my memory still:

> 'I have heard the pigeons of the Seven Woods
> Make their faint thunder, and the garden bees
> Hum in the lime tree flowers; and put away
> The unavailing outcries and the old bitterness
> That empty the heart ...
> I am contented, for I know that Quiet
> Wanders laughing and eating her wild heart
> Among pigeons and bees.'

Yeats, Hyde, and I used to sit up every night until one or two in the morning, talking, it seems to me, about everything and everybody under the sky of Ireland, but chiefly about the theater of which Yeats's mind was full. These were wonderful nights, long nights filled with good talk, Yeats full of plans for the development of the theater. The mornings were devoted to work, the afternoons to out-of-doors, and the evenings to the reading of scenarios for plays, the reading of short plays in English by Lady Gregory and in Irish by Hyde. Lady Gregory and Hyde read out to us from time to time their translations of Irish songs and ballads, in the beautiful English of her books and of Hyde's 'Love Songs of Connacht.' Yeats and Lady Gregory made a scenario of a play and Hyde spent three afternoons 'putting the Irish on it.' She has written how one morning she went for a long drive to the sea, leaving Hyde with a bundle of blank paper before him. When she returned in the evening, Dr. Hyde had finished the play and was out shooting wild duck. This play was 'The Lost Saint.' Dr. Hyde put the hymn in the play into Irish rhyme the next day while he was watching for wild duck beside the marsh. He read out the play to us in the evening, translating it back into English as he went along, and Lady Gregory has written how 'we were all left with a feeling as if some beautiful white blossom had suddenly fallen at our feet.'

At that time I was more interested in Yeats's writing and lyrical poetry and in Hyde's Gaelic revival than I was in Yeats's plans for an Irish theater. Yeats was more interested in the poetry that moves masses of people in a theater and in the drama than in what suffices to make up a book of lyric poetry that might lie on a lady's or gentleman's drawing-room table. I told Hyde and Yeats that that reminded me of Montaigne's[2] saying that he had deliberately put indecencies into his essays because he hated the idea of those essays lying on women's tables.

Lady Gregory was then at work on her two great books, 'Cuchulain of Muirthemne'[3] and 'Gods and Fighting Men.'[4] In these two books she brought together for the first time and retold in the language of the people of the country about her, in the unspoiled Elizabethan English of her own neighborhood, the great legends of Ireland. She did for the old Irish sagas what Malory did for the Knights of the Round Table, and fairly won the right to be known as the Irish Malory.

Another night I first heard the name of John M. Synge. Yeats told us how he had come upon Synge at a small hotel in Paris and persuaded him to come to Ireland, and of the wonderful book[5] that he had written on the Aran Islands. Yeats and Lady Gregory had tried to have it published. I myself offered to pay the expense of making plates for it, but Yeats said that he wanted the book taken on its merits, even if Synge had to wait some years for a publisher.

Synge's debt to Yeats has not, I think, been fully appreciated. It was Yeats who persuaded him to drop the attempt to rival Arthur Symons as an interpreter of Continental literature to England, and to go back to Ireland and live among the people and write of the life that he knew best.

When Synge was writing his plays, poems, and essays he came

often to Coole. Other guests there were George Russell, the poet and writer, Douglas Hyde, 'John Eglinton,'[6] the brothers Fay, George Moore, and Bernard Shaw, and Lady Gregory's home really became a center of the literary life of Ireland of the last ten years.

From this great old house, almost covered by creeping vines, with the most beautiful garden I ever saw, the house in which were stored up so many memories of statesmen, soldiers, authors, artists, and other distinguished people, with its great library, its pictures, statues, and souvenirs gathered from many lands, nestling in the soft climate of the west of Ireland, under the gray skies and surrounded by the brilliant greens and rich browns of west of Ireland landscape, or bathed in the purple glow of the air as the sun declined, I carried away two vivid impressions: first, the realization of a unique literary friendship between the chatelaine and the poet Yeats; and, second, of the gentleness and energy of this woman, the stored-up richness of whose mind in the next eight or nine years was to pour forth essays, stories, farces, historical plays, and tragedies, and translations from Molière[7] and Sudermann,[8] and who has, at the cost of infinite time and pains, proved herself to be, with Yeats, the directing genius of the new Irish drama.

When I would come down to breakfast in the morning, I would be amazed to find that she had already done two hours of writing. Something of her initiative reappeared in her two nephews—the lamented Captain John Shawe Taylor, who brought together the Land Conference that did so much toward the peaceable and friendly settlement of the land question and the changing of land ownership in Ireland; and Sir Hugh Lane, who originated, endowed, and established the Dublin Gallery of Modern Painting, which is, according to the highest authorities, the best European gallery of modern art outside of Paris.

The next year in Dublin I saw a rehearsal of 'The Shadow of the Glen'[9] and other plays in a little hall.[10] The actors were young men and women who worked in the daytime, none of them at that time drawing any pay from the theater. I must admit that I then supposed that this venture would go the way of its innumerable predecessors— endure for a few weeks and then vanish. But I was mistaken. I undervalued the tremendous energy, perseverance, and courage of its leaders, Lady Gregory, W.B. Yeats, and John M. Synge; for it has all through required great patience, and not merely courage but audacity in the face of detraction, false friends, discouragement, and croakings of disaster meeting them from all sides. At no time during these years did either Lady Gregory or Yeats receive a penny of money or a penny of profit from their work for this theater. Douglas Hyde once told me that, apart from his lyric poetry, Yeats's greatest gift to Ireland was the drama. I should add that another gift of Yeats to Ireland was the introduction to the Irish drama of Lady Gregory and John M. Synge.

Ireland now has what it did not have when I first went there—two art centers that all Irishmen may be proud of, the Abbey Theater and the Municipal Gallery of Modern Painting. Some little time ago Bernard Shaw, writing of Dublin, said that he had returned there and had found it just as sleepy as of old, with the same old flies still crawling over the same old cakes in the windows, except for two things, the Modern Art Gallery and the Abbey Theater, which were the things showing an influx of new life.

In Dublin that year I spent several long evenings with Synge. He told me of his wanderings in Europe and of his fondness for the people of the west of Ireland and of the Aran Islands. Synge, like Yeats, was much interested in the problem of style, but in a different way. He knew the language of the Wicklow peasant and of the west of Ireland fisherman and of the Aran and Blasket Islanders. Synge came to his style in the same way that Lady Gregory came to hers, by his knowledge of and sympathy with the people who speak Elizabethan English in the west of Ireland, the English of King James's Bible. When Synge's 'Playboy' was first produced in Dublin, it was hooted for a few nights by a few organized 'patriots' who tried in vain to disprove the reputation that Irishmen are supposed to have of possessing a keen sense of humor. Synge was surprised, but not hurt or even annoyed, at the outburst. He was too much of an artist not to know that some people hate all beauty and that others attack strange beauty that they do not at the first sight understand. His chief fear seemed to be lest the outcry against 'The Playboy' might hurt the theater or endanger the cause of his friends.

The first night that 'The Playboy of the Western World' was given in New York it was preceded by 'The Jail Gate,' which is a mournful play; and when the merry row over 'The Playboy' was at its height, I recalled the words of the Irish chieftain in Chesterton's 'Ballad of the White Horse':

'His harp was carved and cunning,
　His sword was prompt and sharp,
And he was gay when he held the sword,
　Sad when he held the harp.

For the great Gaels of Ireland
　Are the men that God made mad,
For all their wars are merry,
　And all their songs are sad.'

This little company of Irish players and their directors have answered the question that is being so often asked in London and

New York—how to make the theaters a success and yet give nothing that is not good art. They have done this, it seems to me, by courage in keeping to the road they have chosen, by nationality in keeping to the narrow limits to which they bound themselves—'works by Irish writers or on Irish subjects'—and by the deliberate simplicity of staging, by which expense is kept down and they are not driven to put on plays for the sake of profit only.

What lesson can America get from this example?

NOTES

John Quinn, an American lawyer, had been a supporter of the Irish Renascence before the Abbey Theatre was even a name. When the newspaper growlings against *The Playboy of the Western World* were mounting in New York ahead of the Irish Players, a welcome sight when Lady Gregory arrived there on 18 November 1911 was her old friend John Quinn. See Daniel Murphy, 'The Letters of Lady Gregory to John Quinn', Ph.D. dissertation, Columbia University, 1961; and *Complete Catalogue of the Library of John Quinn*, 2 vols. (New York: Anderson Galleries, 1924).

1. Jack B. Yeats (1871–1957), younger brother of W.B. Yeats and Ireland's greatest painter. He was also a playwright of originality and importance. His plays include *Apparitions* (1933) and *La La Noo* (1943). He is also the author of a number of idiosyncratic prose works including *Sligo* (1930), *The Amaranthers* (1936), and *The Careless Flower* (1947). A biography of him by Hilary Pyle was published in 1970 and his collected plays and prose were edited by Robin Skelton in 1971.

2. Michel de Montaigne (1533–92), French author of the *Essays,* which established a new literary form, and an early advocate of a humanistic morality that was in sharp contrast to the religious intolerance of his day.

3. *Cuchulain and Muirthemne* (London: Murray, 1902).

4. *Gods and Fighting Men* (London: Murray, 1904).

5. J.M. Synge, *The Aran Islands* (London: Elkin Matthews; Dublin: Maunsel, 1907).

6. 'John Eglinton', pseudonym of William Kirkpatrick Magee (1868–1961), Irish essayist and poet who appears in George Moore's *Hail and Farewell* and James Joyce's *Ulysses.*

7. Molière, pseudonym of Jean-Baptiste Poquelin (1622–73), dramatist and comic genius who was eventually acclaimed as one of the greatest of all French writers. Lady Gregory was influenced by Molière in her comedies. She also made direct translations of him into 'Kiltartan'. See Lady Gregory, *The Kiltartan Molière* (Dublin: Maunsel, 1910).

8. Herman Sudermann (1857–1928), one of the leading writers of the German Naturalist movement.

9. *The Shadow of the Glen,* by J.M. Synge, was first presented by the Irish National Theatre at the Molesworth Hall, Dublin, on 8 October 1903.

10. Camden Street Hall, Dublin.

She Sat Like a Queen*

WALTER STARKIE

On my return to the Abbey Theatre in 1912 I heard from Joe
Kerrigan, one of the principal actors of the company, the story of
their odyssey in the United States during their 1911 tour, when *The
Playboy* excited riotous scenes in the theatre, especially in New York
and Philadelphia. In the latter city the trouble became more serious,
with the result that the whole cast of *The Playboy* were arrested for
performing 'immoral or indecent plays'. Joe Kerrigan, who had
been playing the part of Shoneen Keogh, gave me a graphic account
of the scene in the court before the magistrate. The first witness for
the prosecution, a publican, said that he had sat out the play until
Shoneen's 'coat of a Christian man' was left in Michael James's
hands. Then he made a disturbance and was ejected from the
theatre. 'I found,' he declared, 'as much indecency in that
conversation as would demoralize a monastery.' His brother, a
priest, however, endured the play to the end, and found that Synge
had committed every one of the sins mentioned in the act. 'We
actors,' said Joe Kerrigan, 'were all raging from the start, but when
that priest started to attack my—that is to say Shoneen Keogh's—
character, I got so mad, Walter, that I bawled out "Oh my God!" The
magistrate then said: "If that man interrupts the Court again, turn
him out," forgetting that he was speaking of a prisoner in the dock! I
declare to God the whole lot of us burst out laughing.'

'What did Lady Gregory say to all this, Joe?'

'She sat amongst us, looking like a queen. She placed all her trust
in our lawyer, John Quinn, who was a tower of strength. You should
have seen her face during the cross-examination of the witness when
Mr Quinn asked the witness if anything immoral took place on the
stage, and the latter replied: "not while the curtain was up!" She
smiled when the same witness, the publican, stated that "a theatre
was no place for a sense of humour!" We won the day hands down,
Walter, for the Director of Public Safety, when he was called, said

*Extracted from *Scholars and Gypsies; An Autobiography* (London: John Murray, 1963)
pp. 84–5.

that he and his wife had enjoyed the play immensely and had seen nothing to shock anybody.'

NOTE

For a note on Walter Starkie see p. 38.

*Shanwalla**

JOSEPH HOLLOWAY

Thursday, April 8, [1915]. ... With all its many faults, *Shanwalla*[1] is the best three-act play Lady Gregory has yet given us. ... The drama was well acted, but Acts II and III fell flat after the high promise of Act I, but loud and continuous applause, with cries for author, followed the ending of the piece, and at last Lady Gregory appeared on the stage, attired in black with a mantilla of lace on her head ... to bow her acknowledgement. *Shanwalla* is melodrama run to waste in a choking tangle of unnecessary words.

Saturday, April. ... Wilson[2] spoke of the *Freeman* critique to Lady Gregory, and she said she supposed Holloway wrote it, and Wilson said I didn't—it was a man named Kelly who did so.

'Well, Holloway had a hand in it anyway, I'm sure,' she said.

Wilson said, 'Yeats and Lady Gregory do love you, Holloway.'

Yeats came to him just now and said, 'I see Holloway again in the house.' And Wilson said, 'He likes the play well.' 'Oh, indeed,' was all Yeats replied on hearing that.

Then Sinclair[3] said to me, 'I think, Holloway, you are the villain of the piece in the Directors' eyes.' ...

Wilson told us of Yeats and Lady Gregory making out the programme for the London season if it came off, and Lady Gregory started by saying they should have no gloomy plays on, and then commenced reading out the plays she considered should be done, starting with Synge's *Playboy* and *Riders to the Sea* and *In the Shadow of the Glen* .... Wilson queried, 'What about gloomy plays?'

'Oh, they must be done,' she said, 'and *Deirdre of the Sorrows* as well.'

*Extracted from *Joseph Holloway's Abbey Theatre: A Selection from His Unpublished Journal 'Impressions of a Dublin Playgoer'*, ed. Robert Hogan and Michael J. O'Neill (Carbondale and Edwardsville: Southern Illinois University Press; London and Amsterdam: Feffer & Simons, 1967) pp. 169–70.

Wilson murmured at this. By then her Ladyship passed on to Yeats and mentioned *Cathleen ni Houlihan* and *On Baile's Strand.*[4] 'Cheerful works also,' Wilson interjected without avail. Again her Ladyship murmured, 'They must go on.'

Then she came to her own work and said to Yeats, 'I suppose *Shanwalla* must go on the opening week.' And Yeats said docilely, 'It must!' Wilson objected, but her Ladyship (who is top dog at the Abbey) said, 'It must!' That ended the matter.

She said to put a query after *Mixed Marriage*[5] and *Patriots,*[6] and Wilson suggested, 'Why not *The Dreamers?*'[7] And she said, 'It isn't a good play; I don't see it.' She supposed they would have to put on one of Boyle's, but she didn't like his plays. But for Sinclair's sake, Wilson might put on *The Eloquent Dempsy*[8] the last week.

NOTES

For a note on Joseph Holloway see p. 32.

1. *Shanwalla* was first produced at the Abbey Theatre on 8 April 1915. The theme is a young wife's return from the dead to defend her man falsely accused of murder.

2. A. Patrick Wilson, the producer of the play.

3. Arthur Sinclair, the actor.

4. The first night of Yeats's *On Baile's Strand* was at the Abbey Theatre on 27 December 1904.

5. The first performance of *Mixed Marriage*, by St John Ervine, was at the Abbey Theatre on 30 March 1911.

6. *Patriots*, by Lennox Robinson, had its première at the Abbey Theatre on 11 April 1912.

7. *The Dreamers*, by Lennox Robinson, was first performed at the Abbey Theatre on 10 February 1915, according to Robinson, and on 2 February according to Malone, Kavanagh, and MacNamara.

8. *The Eloquent Dempsey*, by William Boyle, opened at the Abbey Theatre on 10 January 1906.

Blessed Bridget O'Coole*

SEAN O'CASEY

There she was before him. The lean, wand-like arm of Lennox Robinson had waved her out of her chair in a dark corner of the Abbey Theatre office; waved her out to meet Sean, whose play,[1] at last, had been accepted for production. There she was, a sturdy, stout

*Extracted from *Inishfallen, Fare Thee Well* (London: Macmillan, 1949). Reprinted in *Autobiographies*, II (London: Macmillan, 1963).

little figure soberly clad in solemn black, made gay with a touch of something white under a long, soft, black silk veil that covered her grey hair and flowed gracefully behind half-way down her back. A simple brooch shyly glistened under her throat, like a bejewelled lady making her first retreat, feeling a little ashamed of it. Her face was a rugged one, hardy as that of a peasant, curiously lit with an odd dignity, and softened with a careless touch of humour in the bright eyes and the curving wrinkles crowding around the corners of the firm little mouth. She looked like an old, elegant nun of a new order, a blend of the Lord Jesus Christ and of Puck, an order that Ireland had never known before, and wasn't likely to know again for a long time to come.

The first night was very disappointing, for few came, and only thirteen pounds' worth of tickets were bought; the second night was much better, for it was more than half full; and the third capped the previous two, for the house was packed. Going to the theatre early, Sean enjoyed a look of ecstasy on the Old Lady's face as she stood to watch the people gathering round her little theatre. She ran to him when she saw him, caught his hands in hers, and led him out to see the queues forming a long, long trail right round the famous building. Well, he had done what he had set himself to do seven or more years ago: he had mounted a play of his own on the Abbey stage. Odd, he felt no great elation; no more than he would have felt in the middle, or at the end, of a speech in Irish delivered before a crowd of Gaels. He felt, though, as he stood quiet in the vestibule, that he had crossed the border of a little, but a great, new kingdom of life, and so another illusion was born in his poor susceptible soul. He didn't know enough then that it was no great thing to be an Abbey playwright; and, afterwards, when he knew a lot more, he was glad he had suffered himself to feel no jubilation to mar his future by thinking too much of a tiny success: life remained a mystery to him. He thought, not of what he had done, but of what he had to do in the form and substance of his second play; realising, though unaware of it at the time, that to be a great playwright was a very different thing from merely being one who had had one, two, or even three, plays produced by the Abbey Theatre. Coming out of the theatre, however, he shook himself, thinking in himself that sufficient for the day is the good thing thereof. Some time after, he sent in two one-act plays, *Cathleen Listens In*[2] and *The Cooing of Doves*;[3] the first a skit on the Irish politics of the day, the second full of wild discussions and rows in a public-house. The first play was taken by the Abbey, the other returned, and later was used to form the second act of another play.[4] This was the first shock given to Sean by the selective committee of the theatre, for the second work was definitely better as a play than the first. This was the first jolt he got, but he was to get many more before he was much older, and from the same source, too.

The third play[5] was the biggest success of all, for the theatre was booked out in a few days for the whole week. Lady Gregory began to get young again, for all the weight of her seventy years and more. Hands everywhere were shaking Sean's. After his first play, during the recess, the Abbey Company had engaged the theatre to produce a play of their own selection, to keep themselves from the sin of idleness. The play they chose was Ervine's *Mary, Mary, Quite Contrary*,[6] and Sean went to it as a token of his thanks for what they had done for him in the performance of his two works. He was damned glad he did. There he saw, for the first time, an actor, Barry Fitzgerald, glorifying comedy on the Abbey stage. He had never met the man, and no-one had ever mentioned his name to him. Seething with excitement, when the play ended, Sean ran behind the stage to pour out his enthusiasm into the unwilling ears of the other actors. Fitzgerald's not bad, he was told, when he gets a part that exactly suits him. Not bad? echoed Sean; why, he's a born clown! And, when he went with his third play, he had a suggestion for the cast: Fitzgerald was to play the chief comedy part in it. Mr. Robinson demurred, and mentioned the name of another fine actor, F.J. McCormick, for the part; but Sean held firm for Fitzgerald, knowing in his heart that he, and he alone, could get the arrogant, boozy humour from the character. Fitzgerald himself was very hesitant about taking it on, and Sean, with another member of the Company, Gaby Fallon,[7] who had a very fine understanding of acting, stage and production, spent a long time arguing, demonstrating, and cursing, before Fitzgerald finally could be convinced he would do well in the part.[8] The first night showed Dublin that Fitzgerald stood in the front rank of comedy actors, and Sean and Lady Gregory were delighted.

Letters came asking him for his autograph; he was stopped in the street by levelled fountain-pens and pencils held firm by persons demanding his signature on scraps of paper; notes, bearing dignified addresses on their summits, came from others, announcing that They would be At Home on a certain day, at a precise hour, with a hope, in letters of purest gold, that he would be found among the number knocking nicely at Their big hall doors; and, lastly, a letter from Mr. Robinson inviting him to a monthly dinner furnished by a Thirteen Club (or some name of that kind), with a gilded addendum that W.B. Yeats would be there. The ritual was held in a well-known Dublin restaurant bearing a sturdy poetical name. This invitation couldn't be set aside, for it was one conferring real honour; so, trimly dressed and neat as he could make himself, Sean hurried off to mingle with the elect people of Ireland in a ceremonial meal.

*   *   *

It all bewildered Sean for awhile; but, afterwards, he became certain that the attack[9] was born of no sudden impulse, but was thought of long before the cry came. In it there was no tint of fear for Ireland's honour, the integrity of art, or the dignity of the Irishman. It was aimed at Yeats, and if it obliquely hurt and bothered Sean, all the better. It revealed to Sean for the first time the divisions in Ireland's family of literature. But these things were still in the womb of the future, and, for the moment, Sean knew peace. He had entered places unfamiliar; he had done things he did not yet fully understand; and he was quietly excited about it all. Anyway, he was quite at ease with the Old Lady. They got on grand together. They had many things in common besides the theatre. He loved pictures, and she was brimful of what her nephew, Hugh Lane, had done to diamond-clothe the walls of precious buildings with fair paintings of the men of the day, and with those done by their fathers in the old time before. She loved good books, and Sean felt that he was a little ahead of her there. She saw humour sparkle from things thought to be dead, or dull, and so did he; and they often talked and laughed together over tea in a hotel that overlooked the fair form of Stephen's Green; Sean trying to look at home in the posh place, and succeeding in a way; she eating bun after bun, murmuring that she was very, very hungry; and saying that their talk was lovely; though, best of all, she rejoiced that his plays were forcing queues to stand outside her little theatre, ringing a chime of cheeriness into all their chat. So here was Sean, sober and thoughtful, reading a warm invitation to come a spend a week or two in Coole Park, in Galway; eager to go, but a little nervous at the thought of setting out to visit foreign parts.

The Galway Express left Dublin at 8 A.M. He was to get out at Athenry, the King's Ford, where she would be there to meet him so that they could go together to Gort, and on to Coole Park on her own side-car—she had carefully planned it all out in a previous letter to him.

*   *   *

Sean seized his suitcase, hurried on to the platform, and jumped into the train. Ticket or no ticket, he'd be in Athenry to meet the Old Lady. He was astonished to see the whole crowd follow his example. Sheep, he thought, sheep. In his seat, he thought it odd the way fear took people. He had noticed two priests in the crowd who had been just as fearful and agitated as he was himself, or the old agricultural labourer on his way to Galway who hadn't, maybe, more than his bare fare to bring him there. These would surely have defied the Black and Tans,[10] and yet they shook at the thought of venturing a journey without a ticket, through no fault of their own. When the money was collected, Sean found he had to pay seven and six more than the ticket would have cost; and the labourer found the fare he had only enough to bring him to Athenry. There he would have to get out, and walk the rest of the way to Galway. Sean started help by offering two shillings, and the rest of the kindly passengers added enough to permit the old man to travel on in peace.

There she was waiting for him—a trim, stout, sturdy figure, standing upright and still on the platform, ready to guide him safely down to Gort, grimly patient in the midst of the talkative, quickly-moving crowd. A strange, lone figure she looked in a third-class carriage, stuck tight in a mass of peasants and small farmers, and they with baskets on their laps, or live fowl clutched in their hands; while one woman, young and lively, had a big goose, its legs and wings tied with cord, at her feet, so that it could only gabble, mixing its comic cries with the eager, animated chatter of the crowd.

—Der, said Lady Gregory, suddenly pointing out of a window, der's Craughwell where the police were always half afraid to stir, eating, drinking, and sleeping behind iron doors, thick walls, and steel-shuttered windows. We'll pass Ardrahan later on, remembering what Davis[11] sang,

> And fleet as deer, deh Normans ran
> Tro' Curlew's Pass and Ardrahan.

—An' will again, please God, murmured a quiet voice from a corner.

She has a bit of lisp, thought Sean, and I only after noticing it now. Look at her there, with all her elegance, well at ease among the chattering crowd of common people; so why shouldn't I be steady in my mind at coming to a Big House, among rare silver and the best of china, sleeping in a bounteous bed, and handling divers tools at food never seen before. And he took heart, and felt strong, looking at the calm, handsome old face, smiling at the chatter of the people and the frightened cackling of the fowl. In the main, silent they had to sit, for she was at one end of the carriage and he at the other; so he had time to sort out his tumbling thoughts, watching her, and wondering by what devious ways she of the grandees had managed to come so close to the common people. It's little she's said herself of her younger days, dropping a bare hint, here and there, of what she thought and what she did between residence in Roxborough House, where she was born and lived her youth; and Coole Park, where she lived when she married; and Tullyra Castle, where Edward Martyn, spouse of terror, lived, told his beads, and spent most of his life like a colourless moth, fluttering between the finger and thumb of a friar.

Lady Gregory was the younger child of a large family and held a small corner in the activities surrounding her sisters, the clever Elizabeth, the musical Gertrude, and the beautiful Adelaide, afterwards the mother of Sir Hugh Lane. To the pulsing piston-beat of the hurrying train, Sean pictured her dissolving her own life into the life around her—as we all do—but religiously preserving to herself a secret seed of thought that was to grow into a fine and sturdy understanding of literature; into a shrewd and germinant companionship with Yeats; into a wise and firm Dame Halbardier of the Irish Renaissance; into a lively prop that kept the shaky Irish Theatre standing; into the humorous dramatic writer whose plays will do their devoirs freshly on many a stage, here and elsewhere, for many a year to come.

It is most likely that she played games, went to church twice on Sundays—dwindling into a visit once, if the day happened to be very wet; committed to memory innumerable woeful and winning texts of the Bible; looked over photos of trimly-dressed relatives and friends, set down safe in the thick and gilded pages of an album; some sitting on marble or brocaded chairs, others standing beside Doric pillars, with the whole world behind them; the women floating upward out of balloon-like dresses, beset with a forest of flounces, the men denoting manliness by husky beard or oratorical moustaches. He could see her, at the end of the day, saying her prayers, before she climbed up a ladder on to a heavily-curtained bed, to try to conjure sleep out of stuffy and most respectable air. Perhaps, some night or other, she slid aside the tremendous curtains to get a glimpse of the moon whose golden disk was telling a story of loveliness to the lass of the tenement as well as to the lass of the Big House.

No Peter Pansy came flying in at her window—the curtains were a little too thick for that young mab man—to whisk her off to a never, never, forever land, turning things that were into things that were not; no Winnie the Pooh gambolled in her garden; instead, her fancies were formed from the brown wind of Connacht, in summer soft and sensitive; in winter sending the foam flying frightened from the waves, beating the Galway coast, carrying the spindrift over the land to cover her window with its healthy, bitter brine. And in the midst of the breeze or blast, she learned of the deeds of Cullen's Hound; listening with a wide-open ear to her nurse, Mary Sheridan, telling tremendous tales of him who swore by the oath of his people that *He would make his doings be spoken of among the great doings of heroes in their strength.* So he did, so did she. Has it not been all written down by her in the fine, gay book called *Cuchulain of Murhevna?* It's well Sean could see her, she sitting up in her big bed, her hair chained up for the night, her firm lips half open, her eyes intent on fancied glories that Mary Sheridan's seeding words set out before her: warriors, sages, stately queens, trancing the young girl into seeing Maeve herself, great queen of Cruachen, fixed, fine, and haughty, in the great red-repp chair of Roxborough, and she listening to the rich-bronze chariots of the Red Branch Knights thundering by in the woods outside.

She lived her young life, and rose out of the red-repp and yellowplush life of the time: plush-covered photo-frames, plush-covered bodies and furniture, plush-covered souls full of plush-covered faith in God. That she questioned these things is certain; and that she felt another life, wider, harder, and mightier than her own, around her, is certain, too; for of all those who were with her when her busy literary and dramatic life began, she alone sat among the plain people, safe at ease, while they sat safe at ease with her. With all his scented, elegant Tony Lumpkin life, George Moore rarely had the heart to stray far beyond the border of his Aubusson carpet; and when he did so, got lost, and hurried back to its soft terra firma, giving thanks for a happy deliverance before his holy Manet icon hanging on the wall. Poor, old, clumsy-minded Edward Martyn, lurching round in the shadows of his ta ra ra Gothic house, pumping *Palestrina* out of a harmonium, trying to clap a friar's cowl on the head of life, tried to hide himself in the dim light from a holy candle clamped to his damp and pudgy hand; Yeats, who went through life with ears cocked to hear what no-one else could, heard something strange at times, shown by his letters defending the locked-out workers; didn't like what he heard, shuddered, and turning aside, chanted,

All things uncomely and broken, all things worn out and old,
The cry of a child by the roadway, the creak of a lumbering cart,
The heavy steps of the ploughman, splashing the wintry mould,
Are wronging your image that blossoms a rose in the deeps of my heart.

Shocked he was by this creak and cry, so he started to run, chanting,

Come away, O human child!
To the waters and the wild,
With a faery, hand in hand,
For the world's more full of weeping than you can understand.

But Lady Gregory wasn't afraid of the child's cry or the creak of the lumbering cart; and she stayed to speak warm words to the ploughman splashing the wintry mould. She trotted fearlessly beside all these things, sad or merry; listened to their tales, sang songs with them when they were merry; and mourned with them when a silver cord was sundered or a golden bowl was broken. The taste of rare wine mingled with that of home-made bread on the tip of her tongue; her finely-shod feet felt the true warmth of the turf fire, and beside its glow she often emptied the sorrows of her own heart into the sorrow of others. Out of her plush and plum, she came to serve the people, body and mind, with whatever faculties God had given her.

NOTES

Sean O'Casey (1880–1964), Irish dramatist renowned for realistic dramas of the Dublin slums in war and revolution, in which tragedy and comedy are juxtaposed in a way new to the theatre of his time, and for later plays that use the techniques of Expressionism and Symbolism. His plays include *The Shadow of a Gunman* (1923), *Juno and the Paycock* (1924), *The Plough and the Stars* (1926), *The Silver Tassie* (1928), *Within the Gates* (1934), *The Star Turns Red* (1940), *Red Roses for Me* (1943), *Cock-a-Doodle Dandy* (1949), *The Bishop's Bonfire* (1955), and *The Drums of Father Ned* (1958). Six volumes of autobiography appeared from 1939 to 1956. On the friendship between Sean O'Casey and Lady Gregory see Roger McHugh, 'Sean O'Casey and Lady Gregory', *James Joyce Quarterly*, O'Casey Issue, VIII, no. 1 (Fall 1970) 119–23. See also A.C. Edwards, 'The Lady Gregory Letters to Sean O'Casey', *Modern Drama*, VIII, no. 1 (May 1965) 95–111; Lady Gregory, 'How Great Plays Are Born: The Coming of Mr. O'Casey', *Daily News* (London) (27 March 1926), p. 6; and Elizabeth Coxhead, 'Sean O'Casey', *Lady Gregory: A Literary Portrait*, 2nd ed., revised and enlarged (London: Secker & Warburg, 1966) pp. 183–92. *Lady Gregory's Journals 1916–1930*, ed. Lennox Robinson (London: Putnam, 1946) contains important background material about O'Casey's early plays.

1. *The Shadow of a Gunman* was first presented at the Abbey Theatre on 12 April 1923.

2. *Cathleen Listens In* was first produced at the Abbey Theatre on 1 October 1923.

3. *The Cooing of Doves* was rejected by the Abbey Theatre.

4. *The Plough and the Stars.*

5. The first performance of *Juno and the Paycock* was at the Abbey Theatre on 3 March 1924.

6. This play was not produced at the Abbey Theatre.

7. Gabriel Fallon (b. 1898) joined the Irish Civil Service and worked in London as a young man. In 1920 he returned to Dublin, where he joined the Abbey Theatre Company as a spare time actor (the general practice then) and acted in the first productions of Sean O'Casey's plays. He left the Company in 1928, but remained interested in the theatre as a critic and, since 1959, as a Director of the Abbey Theatre. His writings include *Sean O'Casey: The Man I Knew* (London: Routledge, 1965), *The Abbey and the Actor* (Dublin: The National Theatre Society, 1969), and several articles on the theatre in various periodicals.

8. Captain Jack Boyle.

9. When O'Casey's *The Plough and the Stars* was first performed at the Abbey Theatre on 8 February 1926, it created the most celebrated riot since Dublin playgoers erupted over Synge's *The Playboy of the Western World*. Its obvious censure of methods of revolution angered the diehard Republicans; a small number of men attempted to rush the stage, and police protection had to be sought for the players. The *Irish Times* for 12 February 1926 reported that when the play was at a standstill Yeats shouted at the rioters from the footlights rebuking them: 'Is this going to be a recurring celebration of Irish genius? Synge first, then O'Casey ... Dublin has once more rocked the cradel of genius'.

10. British auxiliary troops in Ireland.

11. Thomas Davis (1814–45), Irish writer and poet who swiftly came to be regarded as *the* national poet, and was the inspiration of the Young Ireland movement.

Where Wild Swans Nest*

SEAN O'CASEY

A long, sweeping drive, left and right, gave a ceremonial pathway to Coole House, which shone out, here and there, in hand-broad patches from between majestic trees, ripe in age, and kingly in their branchiness. The House was a long, yellowish-white Georgian building, simply made, with many windows, while a manly-looking entrance—tightly shut now for a long time—faced what was once a curving expanse of lawn, smooth as green enamel in a rajah's brooch; but was now a rougher, but gayer, gathering of primrose and violet, making themselves at home where once prime minister, statesman, and governor, with their silk-gowned and parasoled women, strolled over the velvety green, their grace, charm, and power manœuvring the poor world about to their own sweet liking.

Lady Gregory was a Connachtwoman, knowing every foot of the province; every story told by every bush and stone in the counties of Galway and Clare; and she showed her Connacht rearing by compelling her seventy-odd years to climb down, like a stiff gazelle, from the high seat of the side-car, running to the threshold of the house, turning, and stretching out her two hands to say, with a beaming smile, One and twenty welcomes, Sean, to the House of Coole!

Mistress of a grand house, dying reluctantly, filled a little too full with things brought from all quarters of the known world; some of them bringing into his fancy the ghosts of a Victorian age, and others, more modern, that would send these ghosts away again, moaning; a huge gleaming marble figure of Andromeda in the drawing-room, brought in from the terrace when it had shocked the finer feelings of the people with its clean, cold nakedness; the really glorious library, walled with precious books in calf and vellum, forgotten, the most of them; unheeded, too, though they still murmured in Sanskrit, Greek, and Latin against the changing tempo of the reading world. Here was a house that for a century and more had entertained great people as well as tinkers and tailors, for every

*Inishfallen, Fare Thee Well (London: Macmillan, 1949). Reprinted in Autobiographies, II (London: Macmillan, 1963).

old or young fiddler, passing through south Galway, came to patronise Coole, receiving praise and largesse after playing, maybe, *Blue Butterfly Dancin'*, *The Soft Deal Board*, or *Pulse of the Bards*, *Awaken*: and as he went up the stairs (the walls covered with engraving and mezzotint so that you passed by, without knowing it, half of England's history) he fancied he heard the dancing notes of *The Red-capped Connachtman* flowing from an old fiddle, mingling with the sonorous voice of Yeats chanting out of him about the wild swans of Coole.

In the library o' nights, heavy curtains pulled taut, a blazing log fire in a huge open grate, Sean stretched out cosy in a deep settee, while she, from the gentle aura of soft candle-light, read him Hardy's Epic-Drama of the war with Napoleon, in three parts, nineteen acts, and one hundred and thirty scenes; read and read till he found himself battling sleepily for dear life to keep himself awake, and be polite to the Spirit of the Years, the Spirit of Pity, the Spirit of Rumour, the Spirits Ironic and Sinister. The poem seemed to have been begun in the dark ages, and he felt that it would roll on till the light of the sun gave out; though he murmured it was all lovely when she paused for breath, cutely conjuring her not to tire herself too much with the dint of the direful reading. But, night after night, she pegged away at it, till the very last word was spoken, and she could murmur, half exhausted, Dat's de end! Two great achievements: one for her—that she survived the reading; the other for him—that he kept awake, though feeling old and grey and full of sleep when she was finished. But, later on, Hardy came to him a far, far greater man than Sean had thought him then.

However, the gentle lady made up for the strain by reading him *Moby Dick* and Hudson's fine *The Purple Land*. Once only did he burst out into protesting: when she, full of enthusiasm, and certain of pleasing him, read a Labour play called *Singing Jail Birds*; to Sean then, to Sean now, the worst play ever written signifying its sympathy with the workers.

Oh, stop, woman, for God's sake! he had bawled, forgetful of where he was, rising, and pacing to the far end of the room: the Labour Movement isn't a mourning march to a jail-house! We are climbing a high hill, a desperately steep, high hill through fire and venomous opposition. All of those who were highest up have dropped to death; lower down, most of the climbers have dropped to death; lower still, many will drop to death; but just beneath these is the invincible vast crowd that will climb to the top by the ways made out by their dear dead comrades!

Perhaps you're right, Sean, she had said, hurriedly putting the book away, something ashamed at having so delightedly praised such an insignificant work.

One evening she came in, aglow with a surprise for Sean—a new petrol lamp into which air was pumped so that, she said, we'll have a light that makes the night even as the day of a sunny summer morning. She stood the lamp on a stand on a high table; and a lovely thing it looked with its silver-like stem and opalescent shade. Lady Gregory's maid, Bridget, hovered round while her ladyship pumped air into the petrol bowl, anxiously watching, and murmuring, Let me handle that, leave it to me, now, me lady, to be answered with the angry and impatient retort of Doh away, doh away, woman; it's twite simple, and I tan handle it myself. Turning to Sean, she added, And now you'll soon see a light dat never was on sea or land.

She was right, too, for as soon as she put a light to it, the thing gave out a mighty hiss that was half a scream, a bluish-white flame shot up high as the ceiling, the old lady's face, panic in her eyes, became as opalescent as the lamp-shade, and her wildly-puckered little mouth began to send frantic and harmless puffs of air towards the soaring, hissing flame, the agitated mouth suddenly opening wide, between the puffs, to shout at Bridget, Bring a blanket, bring a blanket, Bridget, before de house does up in fire! Sean whipped up a rug from the settee, and placed it between their faces and the flame for fear it might explode; and behind this safety-curtain the three of them juggled, blew, and smothered the thing till the fire died down; standing round it on guard till it cooled, and Bridget could safely carry the silver bowl and cracked opalescent bowl out of our sight into the kitchen.

—Oh! murmured her ladyship, sinking down to the softness of the settee, a bunishment for my banity; tinking I could do it alone; tinking I knew too much. Back to de tandles dat bring peace and surety to men of doodwill.

It was strange to see that white, frightened look flash across the face of a brave soul; that fine firm face shrinking from physical fire, though she walked calm through the ordeal of spiritual and mental fire when she fought the good fight for the freedom of the theatre against priest, peasant, and politician, howling loud and long for the putting down of Synge. Against them all she stood, fighting it all out victoriously in Ireland's heart, and dipping deep into the battle again throughout the mighty cities of America, choosing strife that was good rather than the loneliness of a false peace. Again, later on, she defended *The Shewing-up of Blanco Posnet* against Dublin Castle, its robed Lord Lieutenant, its pursuivant, its equerries, men-at-arms, scrolls, parchments, laws and crests, archer Shaw beside her, shooting many a broadcloth stinging arrow of wit into the squirming enemy, making them fall back, and yelp, and lower their banners, and seek shelter in the hollows of the hills of silence.

Again her banner of courage (a gay one, too) had gone up on a day that brought Yeats, Florence Farr, Arthur Symons, and others, to take dinner with her in London. Seeing a letter from home on the table, she took it to another room to read it quiet, finding that every line told of a new disaster, caused by the Big Wind of that year—great lime trees laid flat, oaks, elms, pine, and larch, the calm growth of near a century, had come tumbling down, shattering demesne walls, impeding the public roads; and a tremendous and lovely ilex, the pride of the place, had fallen, given up the ghost, and was no more. But not a word did she say of all this to her guests, but sedately read the play, *Riders to the Sea*, that they had come to hear.

When she got home again, she didn't sit down to wail, but set out on a journey seeking a sawmill, and picked up a second-hand one somewhere; found suitable and unsuitable men to get it going, making all sorts of things for the comfort and convenience of the local people; selling them at cost prices, so cleverly turning an evil into a good thing; the good stretching far, for when Sean came to Coole, the sawmill was still working hoarsely and jerkily, turning out things from the remnants of the fallen timber. And so this brave old Commissar of Galway turned the *Keening of Kilcash* into a busy, surging song of work, though still retaining some of its sadness for the loss of so much upright elegance.

He hadn't been ten minutes at the table before he felt he had often been there, to eat soberly, and talk merrily of books and theatre, and of the being of Ireland; she in simple and most gracious ways showing how things were handled; pointing out that dese things were done, not because of any desire for ceremony, but because dey made one more comfortable, and made things easier to eat. So he was soon at rest, she, when she wanted something from the kitchen, snapping a finger against a tiny Burmese gong that gave a soft, pensive, penetrating note, holding in its quivering sound the muted song and sadness of Burma. Once, after such a meal, they passed through a room where the blue mountains of the Barony of Loughrea nodded in at the great bow-windows; and halting his steps, Sean paused in front of a young, broad-shouldered man with an open and courageous face.

—My dear son, she murmured softly, my dear, dear son, lost leading his air-squadron over de Italian battlefield. For months and months I had dreaded it, for I knew de German planes were well ahead of ours in design and swiftness.

He wished he hadn't paused before the picture. What the hell could he say to her? He gave a quick glance, and saw that holy tears were racing down the wrinkled channels of her cheeks. He touched her old arm softly.

—Dear lady, dear friend, he said, a little savagely, the falling into death of a young, hearty man is a common thing, and may be a more common thing in days to come. The death of youth has been glorified in the damnable beauty of the belief that They will not grow old as we grow old. That is the heresy of age comforting its conscience in its own comfort and continued security. I am, and always will be, against the death of the young. It is for us who are still standing to fight for the deliverance of the young from a youthful death; from the cruel and wasteful banishment of our younger life, with all its lovely and daring visions barely outlined, becoming, when they go, a tinted breath of memory. To the old, death comes as a fair visitor; to the young, death is a savage intruder.

—We must be brave, she said, forcing her head higher; we must fence our sorrow away so that no shadow falls on those left singing and dancing around us. Come, let us doh for a walk in de woods.

The Seven Woods of Coole with their many winding paths, so many that it behoved a rambler to go warily that he be not lost in the mazes among the trees. These were among the beloved walks of Yeats, though Sean never cottoned to them, disliking their gloom, with the weight of gorgeous foliage drooping down, sombre, full of sighs and uneasy rustling, as if God had made them plaintive. Sometimes what Lady Gregory called a badger cut across their path, and red squirrels shot up the trees at their coming, moving on to the ones nearer the orchard so that they might be close to the fruit when the workers went home by the evening star. In her working overalls, which were an old black dress, an older, wide-brimmed, black straw hat, leather gauntlets over her able, wrinkled hands, one of which clutched a keen, chisel-edged stick, the Old Lady walked beside him, or a little before when the going got bad. Here, in the Wood of the Nuts, right in their way, callous and impudent, rose a mighty thistle, fully eight feet high, thrusting out its savage barbs towards their breasts, daring them to come on. Then, with the fire of defiance in her eyes, her ladyship charged down on the foe, hissing angrily, one gauntleted hand seizing a spiked branch, while the other stabbed the main butt of the thistle with the chisel-end of the stick, till the branchy spikes tottered, bent back, and fell to the ground, the victory celebrated by an uplifted stick and a fierce muttering of So perish all de king's enemies!

Occasionally, through the lusty leafage of hazel and ash, they caught a silver glimpse of Coole river flowing by, a river that bubbled up suddenly from the earth in a glade, a lonely corner, alive and gay and luminous with a host of pinkish-blue and deeply-blue and proud forget-me-nots; a secret corner that Lady Gregory had challenged Sean to find, and which had suddenly surrounded him on his third day of searching; a place so lovely in its blossoming loneliness that he felt he should not be there. Not a note from a bird disturbed its quietness; no lover and his lass, even, had passed through this glade; no breeze brought the faint lowing of far-off cattle to his ears; the blue of a serene sky overhead mantling the blue of the flowers at his feet; no sound save the musical gurgling whisper of the water calmly gushing out of the earth; so still, so quiet, so breathless, that Sean thought God Himself might well ponder here in perfect peace; and the merry Mab, in her mimic wagon, might journey home here through the tangled forest of forget-me-nots, without disturbing thoughts of things remembered in tranquillity. This was the river which, after leaving the quietness of God, ran swiftly to widen out into a lovely lake on whose soft bosom wild swans settled and wild swans rose, lifting up the noble head of Yeats to watch them,

> Scatter wheeling in great broken rings
> Upon their clamorous wings,[1]

possibly a little envious of them, and wishing, faintly, he was one because

> Their hearts have not grown old;
> Passion or conquest, wander where they will,
> Attend upon them still.[2]

But Yeats grew old, and cursed the dread handicap of age; yet passion lingered with him to the last, and conquest went before him till he laid himself down in rest to leave us.

Books and trees were Lady Gregory's chief charmers: the one nearest her mind, the other nearest her heart. She laboured long and lovingly in the woods of Coole. She hated rabbits and squirrels only when they nibbled the bark from her young saplings. It was she who first taught Sean to distinguish between the oak—the first dree dat Dod made,—beech, elm, hazel, larch, and pine. She marched along telling their names, the way an eager young nun would tell her beads. Away in a sacred spot of the garden, a magnificent copper beech swept the ground with its ruddy branches, forming within them a tiny dingle of its own. This was the sacred tree of Coole. On its trunk were carved the initials of famous men who had come to visit Coole, so that they might be remembered forever. The initials of Augustus John[3] were there, and those of Bernard Shaw and Yeats were cut deep into the bark that looked like hardened dark-red velvet.

With all her bowing-down before the mystery of poetry and painting, she never left the sober paths trod into roughness by the feet of the common people. One very wet day, she was busy helping to make what was called a Gort cake. When she and Sean returned in a day or so to Dublin, the cake was to be the centre of a tea given in the Green Room of the Abbey Theatre. She usually brought one up for the actors when she visited Dublin. A lot of the actors and actresses elected to regard the cake with contempt; but they ate it all right, and when the tea was done, though the cake would feed a regiment, he had noticed that there was little left behind. The cake was a rich thing of spice, raisins, and currants, but the rarest thing in its make-up was a noggin of brandy to help to damp the dough.

Sean was standing before one of the great bow-windows, watching the rain slashing down in silvery sheets over the saturated lawn, and listening to the sighs of the big lime tree bending discontentedly before the sharp and bitter wind blowing its branches to and fro. Suddenly, through the mist of the rain, he saw a dark figure, crouching to fight the wind and the rain, battling his way up the circling drive to reach the Big House.

—Derrible day, Sean, said Lady Gregory, coming in to have a look out of the window; derrible day!

—Whoever's coming up the drive, Lady Gregory, must feel what you say to be true.

—Oh! It's Sammy Mogan toming to det pension papers signed, she said, staring gloomily at the figure struggling onwards. De foolish man to tome on a day like dis; de foolish man!

She was gone in a second. He heard the bell of the side door ring; heard someone entering the hall, and then a long silence came. Tired of watching the rain, he strolled about staring at the pictures hanging on the stairway wall. Out comes an old man to the hall, muffled up in a big coat, eyes and ears only apparent, a bundle of soppy clothes under an arm, and he bidding her ladyship goodbye at every step.

—You must never tome out on a day like dis aden, Sam, murmured her ladyship.

—What signifies it, me Lady? What's in it for a day but a harmless sup o' rain? Goodbye, now, me Lady. Penethratin' though th' rain is, it treats th' skin quietly, like th' tender touch of a mother bird's wing reachin' over th' nest of her young ones. Well, me lady, goodbye now. An' isn't th' cordial you've just given me afther liftin' me into thinkin' th' heaviest rain on the cowldest day to be no more than the tired leaves fallin' from the high-born branchy trees. Goodbye, me Lady, for with the form signed safe in me pocket, it's whistlin' I'll be all th' way home, intherspersed with prayers for seven blessin's seven times a day on you and all your house. Goodbye, me Lady.

—Whisper, Sean, said Lady Gregory, as they went back to the fire in the library, de Gort cake will lack its warm life dis time. Sam Mogan was so perished wid de wet and cold dat I poured de naggin of brandy into him to bring him back to life.

Sitting in the long and handsome garden, he saw the sun going down behind the grey garden wall and beyond the Hills of Burren, giving Coole a crimson and gold salute before it went. He realised that Lady Gregory, in the midst of her merriment and mourning, was ever running round, a sturdy little figure in her suit of solemn black, enlivened by gleaming eyes and dancing smile; ever running in and out of Yeats's Keltic Twilight, which she could never fully understand; turning his Rose Alchemica into a homely herb; and turning the wildness of his Red O'Hanrahan into the serious, steady dancing of a hornpipe on the Abbey stage. In her humorous and critical moods, swinging a critical lantern, she trespassed into A.E.'s amethystine no-man's-land where A.E. became delirious with quivering, peacock-tinted visions, seeing things innumerable and unmentionable, beings plumed, from pituitary gland to backside, with red, white, green, blue, and orange flames. There he sat, with notebook in hand, taking down divine orders of the day from brother-selfs, master-souls, ancient-beauties, elfs and faeries, madly dancing a rigadoon a dad a derry o. Here she'd trot forward impudently, pulling aside A.E.'s twilight curtains, half hiding the Pleroma, gone today and here tomorrow; disturbing the dusky grandeur of the Great Breath's breathing, and frightening away the dim moths of twilight trees, twilight hills, twilight men, and twilight women, by crying out in her quiet, determined way, through all the mumbo-jamboree of twilight thought, that there were things to cook, sheets to sew, pans and kettles to mend.

It was hard for Sean to single out the best work done by this old woman, flitting through life like a robin with the eye of a hawk; for she had as much to do with what she did not do as she had with what she did; whether it was the writing of plays, or the lofty encouragement (not forgetting the blue curtains for the windows of his little flat) given to Yeats, making the poet at home in the dignity, comfort, and quiet of a fine house; soothing him with a sunny seat under a spreading catalpa tree in a flower-lit garden, where a summer evening was full of the linnet's wings; whether it was the warm determined will that gave her little theatre a local habitation and a world-wide name; for not Yeats, nor Martyn, nor Miss Horniman gave the Abbey Theatre its enduring life, but this woman only, with the rugged cheeks, high upper lip, twinkling eyes, pricked with a dot of steel in their centres; this woman only, who, in the midst of venomous opposition, served as a general run-about in sensible pride and lofty humility, crushing time out of odd moments to write play after play that kept life passing to and fro on the Abbey stage.

On a stone wall surrounding what was once, maybe, a meadow, Sean sat one day simmering in the sun. All over the heath, the crowds of wild waste plants were covered with wide mantles of brilliant-blue butterflies. Never had he imagined such a host of blue evanescent divinity. In the formal garden, here and there, one, or maybe a pair, flew about from this flower to that one, but here they were in tens of thousands. As they settled and rose, they looked like a multitude of

tiny blue banners carried by an invisible army. Or the bright blue
mantle of St. Brighid down from the sky, fluttering near the half-
remembered things of earth. How delightful the sturdy black figure
of her ladyship would look doing a slow, graceful, if a little stiff,
minuet among the brilliant-blue fluttering things. Sean wondered if
Yeats had ever set eyes on these. Hardly, for they were off the beaten,
formal track of his strolling: garden, lake, woods were as far as he
got; and so the gurgling rise of the river and these brilliant-blue
angels of an hour were denied the lyric their loveliness commended.

She loosened the tautness of her own work by taking too much
time helping others, Sean thought as he sat on the wall, encircled
with the cloud of blue butterflies. She became foster-mother to some
plays of Yeats, weaving in dialogue for *Cathleen ni Houlihan* and his *Pot
of Broth*;[4] helping in the construction of *The King's Threshold*[5] and *Where
there is Nothing*,[6] throwing in, for good measure, scenarios from which
Douglas Hyde made *The Poorhouse*[7] and *The Marriage*.[8] In the theatre,
among the poets and playwrights, herself a better playwright than
most of them, she acted the part of a charwoman, but one with a star
on her breast. Ay, indeed, this serving eagerness of hers was a
weakness in her nature. She thought too much of the work of others,
foaming with their own importance, leaving her but little time to
think of her own. So signs on it, a good deal of what she did shows
hurry, hinting in its haste that no matter if mine be not good so long
as that of others be better.

Once troubled with the pushful realism of the younger writers, she
started to write a romantic play around Brian Boru, called *Kincora*.
She made many false starts, but kept hammering away, in spite of
Yeats's advice to give it up; and, though the play got its share of
applause, it wasn't in itself, she says, the success it might have been,
and so hindered a welcome from critic and audience. Give it up! No
wonder it wasn't the success it might have been. Why didn't Yeats
mind his own business! A pity the woman was so near to Yeats while
she was writing the play: he had a bad effect on her confidence in her
own creation. She was concerned with him and her play; he
concerned only with himself. He had no right to tell her to give up
writing the play; but she served so frequently in so many common
ways that Yeats easily dismissed from his mind her natural vigour in
the creation of imaginative drama. It was a shame that the modelling
of the play should have been chilled by a scornful wave of a delicate
hand from a poetical mind that so often dismissed everything save
what was dissolving in the wonder of his own thought.

Lady Gregory had her own Three Sorrows of Storytelling; three
sorrows that were rifling her heart when Sean first came across her,
and founded a friendship with Coole. The tumbling, burning death
of her son, Major Robert Gregory, on the battlefield of Italy, was but

being softened slowly by her transferred devotion to his three young children. His death, too, was a loss to Ireland, for to his many qualities he added that of a fine and sensitive designer for the theatre. In the play, *Kincora*, the king's Great Hall was shown by the hanging of vivid green curtains; there were shields, embossed with designs of gold, upon the walls, and heavy mouldings over the doors. For Brian's tent at Clontarf, a great orange curtain filled the background, with figures standing out against it in green, red, and grey. In *The Shadowy Waters*, he made the whole stage the sloping deck of a galley, blue and dim, the sails and dresses were green, and the ornaments all of copper. When Robert Gregory fell on the hilly soil of Italy, Ireland may have lost an Irish, and more colourful, Gordon Craig.

The Second Sorrow was the Atlantic weaving with her waves a winding-sheet for Sir Hugh Lane, her nephew, when he went down in the *Lusitania*, almost within view of his birthplace in the county of Cork. He it was who, through heavy opposition, gave many gems of painting to many galleries, scattering these lovely things all over Dublin, as another would scatter rose-petals about in the heat of a carnival. A loss he was, a great loss to his people, though only a very few felt it, besides the lonely woman in her home at Coole. To Sean, then, he was none; he felt it not; knew it not; but he knew it well now.

The Third Sorrow was the taking away of the Lane pictures from Dublin by the then British Authorities. A scurvy trick, one of the many done by British authority on Ireland. The lousiest and meanest of robberies ever perpetrated by one country on another. To her last breath, she followed after them, seeking them, seeking them, and often Sean had gone with her. They are still exiled from their native land; but they will be brought back. Though many in Ireland were blind to their beauty, so were others, better placed than the Irish to recognise their loveliness; for one of them, Renoir's *Umbrellas*, lay for a long time deep in the cellar of the National Gallery, too trivial, as the big shots thought, for a hanging on a respectable wall. A scurvy trick, England!

What shall we bring to the place where she now lies asleep forever? Easy enough to answer; easy enough: A promise not to forget the Lane pictures; some of the shining forget-me-nots from the glade where the fresh river rises; a branch from the copper beech that bore the initials of those who had sat at her table and walked in her garden; an old fiddler to play *The Blackberry Blossom*; a butterfly from the gorgeous blue swarm that clouded the heath, like the blue mantle of Brighid, behind the House of Coole; a vine leaf, or two, in token of her gay heart; since she elected to live and die a Christian, a cross; and the voice of her poet-friend chanting:

Here, traveller, scholar, poet, take your stand
When all those rooms and passages are gone,
When nettles wave upon a shapeless mound
And saplings root among the broken stone;
And dedicate—eyes bent upon the ground,
Back turned upon the brightness of the sun
And all the sensuality of the shade—
A moment's memory to that laurelled head.[9]

All the rooms and passages are gone,[10] and saplings root among the broken stone, for an elevated Irish Government has broken down the House and levelled it smooth for nettles to grow upon a shapeless mound. Oh! a scurvy act for an Irish Government to do on the memory of one who was greater than the whole bunch of them put together and tied with string. The god-damned Philistines![11]

NOTES

1. W.B. Yeats, 'The Wild Swans at Coole', *The Wild Swans at Coole* (1919).

2. Ibid.

3. Augustus John (1878–1961), British painter, muralist, and print-maker, known primarily for his portraits, which vigorously characterised many of the political and artistic luminaries of his time. See Michael Holroyd, *Augustus John* (London: Heinemann, 1975). When O'Casey left Dublin for London in 1926 he made friends with Augustus John. The present editor owns two O'Casey first editions presented by the author to Augustus John: *Two Plays: Juno and the Paycock & The Shadow of a Gunman*, inscribed by O'Casey to Augustus John 'with affection for a great artist & great man'; and *Within the Gates: A Play in Four Scenes*, inscribed by O'Casey to Augustus John 'in memory of the magnificence of *Galway* in the Tate Gallery'.

4. *The Pot of Broth* had its première by the Irish National Theatre at the Camden Street Hall on 4 December 1902.

5. *The King's Threshold* was first performed by the Irish National Theatre at the Molesworth Hall on 8 October 1903.

6. *Where There is Nothing* later became *Unicorn from the Stars*.

7. *The Poorhouse* opened at the Abbey Theatre on 3 April 1907.

8. *The Marriage* was first presented at the Abbey Theatre on 16 November 1911.

9. W.B. Yeats, 'Coole Park, 1929', *The Winding Stair and Other Poems* (1933).

10. The House of Coole stood empty for a good many years, and then was sold by the Forestry Department to a contractor, who demolished it for the value of the building stone. The knocker of the front door was presented as a keepsake to the Abbey Theatre green room, and the handsome brass-knob to Bernard Shaw. It may seen by National Trust visitors to Shaw's Corner at Ayot St Lawrence.

11. Sean O'Casey wrote to the *Irish Times* (Dublin) on 6 March 1942: 'This is a sad fate for such a house, so different from the House of Usher. One would think they would have made it into a local Galway Art Gallery, preserving half the history of the places around it. They have done more to embalm the deeds of others, not a tenth as good as Lady Gregory was to Ireland.'

A Visit to Coole Park*

HALLIE FLANAGAN

From the loveliness of South Ireland, and the stern beauty of North Ireland, I travel westward into the primitive. The rolling green hills, the streams in flowering meadows, the thatched cottages with clothes blowing gayly on the hedges, give way to a treeless landscape of furze and stocky shrubs. Stone everywhere now, stone walls, often fallen into decay, stone castles eyeless and dark, stone fences around hard fields, whole villages of stone, strange villages—Mullingar and Athlone. Green gives way to gray, the gray of sod houses and peat bogs, the gray of encircling mountains, with the beat of the sea not far distant, and the somber sky overhead.

At Ballinsloe a boy of about ten gets on. He has the high color, the vivid blue eyes, the arrestingly beautiful face so often seen in Ireland, and he sits very still clutching a brown paper parcel in a small lean hand. He says he is going to Gort, and when I ask, 'For a visit?' he says, 'No, for keeps.' He looks rather pitiful to be going anywhere by himself for keeps, but he explains with a touch of pride, 'The throuble it got me father an me two brithers, an now there is no one at all, for me mither's mind is not what it should be, what with the throuble an all. So it's to Gort I'm goin', to a situation.' Just then we reach Gort, and I can only say, 'I'm sorry,' to which he responds, 'A good luck to ye,' with a brilliant smile which still returns to me at unexpected moments.

At Gort I am met by Lady Gregory's old coachman, who tucks me into the decorative jaunting car, wraps me in colored rugs, and entertains me on the ride to the Park with tale after tale of hunts and house parties in the gay days 'before Master Robert went away to the war.' 'Well I remember when the news came Master Robert was decorated with the Legion of Honor in France,' he says. 'Every man in Gort put on his best and sent some sort of a present to the big house; and there was a bonfire in the square and a celebration indeed, for not a man in Gort but was proud of Master Robert. Such a one he was to pass the time of day with everyone, much like my lady .... But after that it was no time at all until word came he was killed in Italy, and then such a sadness in Gort as we have not got over yet, for not a man or woman in Gort that is not beholden to my lady, and

*Shifting Scenes of the Modern European Theatre (New York: Coward, McCann & Geoghegan, 1928) pp. 35–43.

fond of Master Robert, besides.'

As we enter the gates of the Park we are in great avenues of trees, the seven woods of Coole stretching away to the left, orchards to the right, a long archway of holly and oak evergreen sweeping up to the slope where the old gray house, generous in outline, waits. Lambs are playing on the lawn, a flight of swans rises from the lake, and, waiting by the portico, her black lace shawl blown about her welcoming face, stands Lady Gregory.

We go into the library, a room noble in proportion, rich in temper, with books from floor to ceiling on three sides, the fourth side opening on the Park. A fire of peat and holly branches lights the portraits of bygone Gregorys. It is a warm room, a living room, of the present, yet full of the past. It has the wisdom of a room in which great men of five generations have gathered. Portraits with inscriptions are here of Robert Browning, and Theodore Roosevelt, of Mark Twain, and Bret Harte. 'With Mark Twain one always had the most serious discussions,' said Lady Gregory, 'for like most people who write humorously, Mark Twain was deeply philosophical. Bret Harte would thrill one with tales of America; he believed that the west of Ireland, like the west of America, was a man's country.'

Among Americans at Coole Park, Lady Gregory mentions Mr. and Mrs. George Pierce Baker,[1] asking with great interest about the expansion of the Harvard 47 Workshop into the Yale Theatre. 'Wonderful America,' is her comment, 'to recognize his genius—we won't say for teaching people to write plays, for he and I agree that that is impossible—but for placing people in an environment where their early plays can be discussed, criticised, and given the acid test—production.'

Before Lady Gregory's fireplace for the past twenty years, poets, dramatists, painters, have gathered to talk of Ireland and of art, to read aloud to one another plays and poems in the making.

'I remember the evening when Synge read *Riders to the Sea*,' she said. 'It was a stormy night, with the lake beaten into spray, with rain lashed against the panes. Yeats was here and, I think, Æ. Since the day when I first met Synge wandering among the peasants on the Aran Islands and resented his intrusion (I afterwards learned he resented mine!) we had become great friends. Largely through the influence of Yeats he was turning aside from the rather imitative writing of his Paris days, and was writing of the Islanders. On this night he sat by the fire, bent over, frowning, and read as was his custom, without expression. The room grew instantly still. For the entire twenty minutes we scarcely breathed. When he finished we could not speak. He sat bowed down in his chair, forgetting us. And we sat forgetting everything except Ireland, and the sea, and the sadness of human life.'

There is a sense of leisure at Coole Park. The days are unplanned, free for walks and talks, for solitude, for the unexpected. There are mornings in the sunny breakfast room with its gay collection of

'The theatre of art must discover grave and decorative gestures such as delighted Rossetti and Maddox Brown, and grave and decorative scenery that will be forgotten the moment an actor has said, "It is dawn." The theatre began as ritual and it cannot come to its greatness again without recalling words and gestures to their ancient sovereignty.'

We walk through the greenhouses, Lady Gregory carrying a basket and pruning shears and stopping to show me favorite shrubs and vines, and, as we walk through the grounds, pointing out the growth of acres of trees which she herself planted.

'It was here by the summer house that the idea of the Abbey Theatre was born. We sat here and talked as we often did of our effort, especially of the work of Yeats and Douglass Hyde, to restore the ancient spiritual beauty of Irish legend. Yeats had written a play and Edward Martyn had written one, and I said "We'll have to organize a theatre to get them produced!" The theatre was organized then and there, and the first rehearsal took place, as many early rehearsals did, here in the garden.'

We stroll along the flower-bordered path and sit in the sunshine Staffordshire china figures, amusing miniature Victorias, Garibaldis, O'Connells; and its portraits of Burke and other Irish statesmen who were family friends. There are walks in the garden with Mrs. Robert Gregory, whose conversation is as original and vigorous as her work in illustration and painting. There are voyages of exploration and discovery with Mrs. Gregory's two young daughters, Ann and Catherine, who are filling vacation days with gardening and horse back riding.

Memorable the hours spent in Lady Gregory's salon adjoining the library, a gracious room with exquisite statues set among ferns, a richly personal place with shelves of books inscribed to her, with portraits and miniatures of friends, and paintings of Coole Park by artists who have shared its beauty. At the desk drawn up by the window facing the Park *The Workhouse Ward* was written and *The Rising of the Moon* and many other plays, as well as *Gods and Fighting Men, Visions and Beliefs*, and *The Life of Hugh Lane*.

Here Lady Gregory shows me portfolios of the early days of the Abbey, copies of the Samheim [sic]?, their theatre magazine, old programs amusingly embellished by cartoons and limericks, press clippings of the American tour in 1911. There are many sketches for design and costumes and many caricatures done by Jack Yeats, W. B. Yeats, Æ.

'The problem of design was from the first a difficult one. We were in the days of realism, yet some of us felt that realism was not right

for the Irish plays, particularly for the faery plays. I remember the
storm of dissent caused by Yeats's article on design written in 1899.
near the great autograph tree, and Lady Gregory tells me stories of
the men whose names are engraved there: George Bernard Shaw,
Lord Dunsany, Augustus John, Masefield. The freshest carving is that
of Sean O'Casey. 'My youngest,' smiles Lady Gregory, 'and
sometimes I think my most exciting. You see, not so very long ago
Sean O'Casey was working as a day laborer, sometimes on the roads,
sometimes in factories. He had never had a day's schooling and could
not read nor write, though he had in his possession a box of books
left him by a father he cannot remember but who was, I suspect, a
man of learning. One day Sean heard two men quarreling over a
point in Irish history and one said, "If the one or the other of us
could read now, we could settle it." "Would such as that be in a
book?" asked Sean, and set about teaching himself to read. He began
on the book at the top of the box, which happened to be Locke *On
Human Understanding*. Not exactly a text book for a beginner, but it
proved effective. By the time Sean was twenty he was reading
everything he could lay hands on. One night he dropped in at the
Abbey Theatre, saw his first play, and resolved to write one. The
manuscript came in so carelessly scrawled on scraps of paper that it
was difficult to read it, but I felt in it a flash of power. I had it typed in
order to judge it more fairly, but in this form it was even more
impossible. I took it back, told him that it showed a gift for making
people talk as people do talk, and asked him to rewrite it. The
revision took him a year. When we read it and saw that it wouldn't
do, I think that I was as distressed as he was. Fortunately, being Irish,
he added rage to distress, and swore he would get a play on in spite of
us. The result was *The Shadow of a Gunman* which we at once produced.
Then came *Juno and the Paycock*, and *The Plough and the Stars*, and there
will come others, for I think he has not yet reached his full power.'

On a rainy afternoon Ann and Catherine pick apples in the
orchard, for they are packing a box of the choicest to send to George
Bernard Shaw, their favorite of all the guests who frequent Coole
Park. They tell me with amusement how Shaw was lost in the woods
near the lake. He strolled off in the morning and didn't come back
for luncheon, nor for tea, nor for dinner, and it was well past dark
when the searching party found him. 'Of course he wouldn't ever
admit that he was really lost, but he never teased us again about
seeing something in the woods—because after that, he knew.'

I imagine he did ... For how it may be in sunshine I do not know,
but I am sure that on a gray day when the swans are motionless on
the lake and the air silent save for the drip of rain through green
branches, the seven woods at Coole are full of presences. The moss-
covered rocks are beasts, men, and gods under enchantment. The

myriad, upspringing brown trunks set free imprisoned spirits of the soil. The druid altar, in a shadowy entanglement of vine is not without its sacrifice. Faery rings are here, and faery mounds, and everywhere the splendor of Deirdre, for whom men have died and by whom men live.

Out of communion with the living silence of the woods at Coole Park, poetry, drama, and painting have been born. To walk there is to be stirred by thoughts beyond the reaches of our souls.

Evenings at Coole Park are rendezvous before the fire. Everyone returns from wanderings actual or spiritual and brings what treasure he has found as offering. There is criticism, wise, humorous; instant recognition of the thing attempted; intuitive suggestion, inspired flash of praise. Above all there is an atmosphere of creation, whether Lady Gregory is playing games with Ann and Catherine, whether she is telling of some village happening, or reading aloud, her voice peopling the dim room with folk from a Gaelic Saga.

Lady Augusta Gregory has created more than bears her name. She is of the women who achieve through men. She is wiser than her wisest book, she is more beautiful than the beauty dedicated to her.

NOTES

Hallie Flanagan (1890–1969), American stage director, who served as the national director of the Federal Theatre Project of the Work Projects Administration in 1935–9. Under her leadership, the Federal Theatre staged more than 1,000 productions throughout the United States.

1. Professor George Pierce Baker (1866–1935), who made reputation as teacher of dramatic composition in his course in playwriting. See Wisner Payne Kinne, *George Pierce Baker and the American Theatre* (Cambridge, Massachusetts: Harvard University Press, 1954).

2. *Samhain*, the organ of the Irish Literary Theatre, ran from October 1901 to November 1908. It was edited by W. B. Yeats.

Index

Page numbers followed by the letter n indicate that the reference is to a note.

Abbey Theatre
  disturbances during first production of
    The Playboy, 33–9, 41n, 72, 83
  first night suppers, 28, 29
  origins, 32n, 49, 72
  repertoire and season, 50
  selection of plays, 44
Abbey Theatre Company, 51, 67, 73, 77
  American tour, 45n
  origins, 49, 56, 72, 108
  school of acting, 50, 67
AE, see Russell, George
Allgood, Sara, 75, 77n
Arabi and His Household, 7n
Arliss, George, 67, 70n
Armonde Dramatic Society, 31n
Arnold, Sir Edwin, 9, 12n
Ave, 7n, 8

Baker, George, 65, 66n, 70, 107, 110n
Balzac, Honoré de, 11, 13n
Basterot, Count, 15
Beardsley, Aubrey, 6n
Ben Bulben, 14
The Bending of the Bough, 12n, 59n, 64
Benson, F.R., 64
Best, Dr Richard, 38n, 39n
Birthright, 47, 48n, 60n
Blavatsky, Madame, 40, 41n
Blunt, Wilfred Scawen, 7n, 41n
Boru, Brian, 29, 31n, 103
Boyle, William, 58, 60n
Bridie, James, 30, 31n
Browne, Maurice, 76n
The Building Fund, 60n

Cathleen Listens In, 88n
Cathleen ni Houlihan, 5, 7n, 23, 29n, 73, 87
  played by Lady Gregory, 27, 29n
  plot, 74n
The Clancy Name, 60n

La Comédie Humaine, 13n
Confessions of a Young Man, 5n
The Cooing of Doves, 88
Coole Park
  autograph tree, 21, 100, 109
  destroyed, 105
  the Seven Woods, 21, 22, 99, 100,
    109–10
  visited by:
    Bernard Shaw, 109
    George Moore, 1–4
    Hallie Flanagan, 106–10
    John Quinn, 79–82
    John Synge, 107
    Sean O'Casey, 95–103
    Signe Toksvig, 18–25
    W.B. Yeats, 1–5, 10, 13–15
The Countess Cathleen, 2, 10, 55, 62
Court Theatre, London, 40, 65
The Courting of Emer, 12
Cuchulain of Muirthemne, 10, 64, 81

Deirdre [AE], 31
Deirdre [Yeats], 31, 32
Deirdre of the Sorrows, 40, 86
Devaney, John, 24
Devorgilla, 30, 31n
Diarmuid and Grania, 1–4, 6n, 64
Disraeli, 68, 69, 71n
Dooney Rock, 14
The Dreamers, 87
Dublin Dramatic School, 31n
The Dynasts, 96

Early Eastern Christianity, 15
Edgeworth, Maria, 59, 60n
The Eloquent Dempsey, 87
Erin, 13n
Esther Waters, 5n

Faerie Queen, 4

Fallon, Gabriel, 89, 94n
Fay, Frank J., 31n
Fay, William George, 31n
Fitzgerald, Barry, 89
Flanagan, Hallie, 110n
Frohman, Charles, 64, 66n

Gaelic League, 45n, 56
Gaiety Theatre, Manchester, 51n
The Gaol Gate, 73, 74n
Gods and Fighting Men, 81
Gonne, Maud, 29n
Gort barm-brack, 28, 29, 38, 100, 101
Gregory, Ann, 108, 109
Gregory, Catherine, 108, 109
Gregory, Lady Isabella Augusta
    advice on establishing Little Theatre
        movement, 75, 76
    boycotted by local council, 39, 40
    collaborating in writing *Diarmuid*, 6n
    collecting folk legends, 14, 17n
    considered as political leader-writer,
        41n
    Cuchulain legends, 10–12
    death, 17n
    defends Irish plays from American
        critics, 42, 47, 48, 71
    described by:
        George Moore, 2, 4, 9
        Maire Nic Shiubhlaigh, 28
        Sean O'Casey, 88
        Signe Toksvig, 19
    first interest in drama, 27, 28
    first meeting with John Synge, 107
    first meeting with Sir William Gregory,
        12n
    first meeting with Yeats, 16n
    in role of *Cathleen ni Houlihan*, 27, 29n
    influence of Molière, 84n
    influence of Yeats, 80, 103
    influence on Yeats, 2, 4, 5, 10, 14, 17n,
        79, 80
    interest in music halls, 67, 68
    'Kiltartan' dialect, 5, 6n, 84n
    learns Gaelic, 63
    murder threat during American tour,
        45n
    sketch by Augustus John, 19
    translating folk tales, 43
    visit to Egypt, 7n
Gregory, Mrs Robert, 108
Gregory, Robert, 30
    awarded Legion of Honour, 106
    death, 98, 103
    designing scenery, 30, 104

Gregory, Sir William, 7n, 8, 9, 12n
Gwynn, Stephen, 31n

Hail and Farewell, 5n
Hardy, Thomas, 96
Healey, Archbishop, 73
The Heather Field, 6n, 59n
Henderson, W.A., 31, 32n
Henley, William, 40, 41n
Hippolytus, 76
Holloway, Joseph, 32n, 86
Horniman, Annie, 32n, 49, 51n, 66
Hugh Lane's Life and Achievement, 6n, 24
Hyacinth Halvey, 47
Hyde, Douglas, 42, 45n, 56, 64, 78, 80, 81

The Image, 40, 41n
In the Shadow of the Glen, 47, 48n, 84n, 86
Irish dramatic movement, origins, 56
The Irish Homestead, 39n
Irish Literary Theatre, 6n, 17n, 28, 55
Irish National Theatre Society, 17n, 28,
    29n, 31n, 32n, 64
Irish Players, *see* Abbey Theatre
    Company

John, Augustus, 19, 105n

Kerrigan, Joe, 85
'Kiltartan' dialect, 5, 6n, 84n
Kincora, 29, 30, 31n, 103
King Guaire of Connaught, 25, 26
The King's Threshold, 32n, 105n
Krans, Horatio, 62

Lacy, Mrs, 31n
Lahey, Mgr, 73
The Lake, 5n
Lane, Sir Hugh, 16, 17n, 24, 82, 91, 104
The Last Feast of the Fianna, 64
Layard, Sir Austen, 40, 41n
Lecky, William, 9, 12n
Lever, Charles, 59, 60n
The Light of Asia, 9, 12n
Literary Theatre, *see* Irish Literary
    Theatre
Little Theatre movement, 76n
The Lost Saint, 81
Lover, Samuel, 59, 60n
Lusitania, 24, 104

McCormick, F.J., 89
McDonough's Wife, 44, 46n
Maeve, 6n, 64
Magee, Ethne, 52, 53

Martyn, Edward, 2, 6n, 7n, 12n, 16n, 18.
    64, 91, 93
Mary, Mary, Quite Contrary, 89
Meyer, Kuno, 11, 12, 13n
Milligan, Alice, 64
Mixed Marriage, 58, 60n, 87
A Modern Lover, 10, 12n
Molesworth Hall, 32
Molière, 84n
Montaigne, Michel de, 81, 84n
Moore, George, 5n, 6n, 12n, 64, 93
Morris, William, 40, 41n
A Mummer's Wife, 10, 12n
Muncke, Norman, 66
Municipal Gallery, Dublin, 25, 82, 83
The Municipal Gallery Revisited, 33n
Murray, Thomas C., 47, 58, 60n, 64

Nassau Hotel, 28
Nietzsche, Friedrich, 80

O'Casey, Sean, 94n, 109
On Baile's Strand, 87
Our Irish Theatre, 6n

Parker, Louis, 71n
Patriots, 87
Persse, Adelaide, 24, 91
Persse family, 8, 91
The Playboy of the Western World, 40, 63, 86
    American tour, 42, 45n, 52–5, 59, 70–3,
        83, 85
    censored, 55
    disturbances during first production,
        33–9, 41n, 72, 83
    plot, 33n
The Plough and the Stars, 94n

Quinn, John, 65, 84n, 85

Raftery [poet], 23, 78
Reminiscences of Impressionist Painters, 5n
Riders to the Sea, 86, 107
The Rising of the Moon, 73, 74n
Robinson, Lennox, 58, 59n, 64
Russell, George, (AE), 39n, 102

Saints and Wonders, 26
Samhain, 110n
The Savoy, 2, 6n
The Secret Rose, 5, 10
The Shadow of a Gunman, 109
The Shadowy Waters, 1, 3, 4, 6n, 10
Shanwalla, 86, 87
Shaw, George Bernard, 45, 66n, 69, 70,
    109

Shawe-Taylor, Mrs Elizabeth, 8
Shawe-Taylor, John, 16, 82
The Shewing Up of Blanco Posnet, 55, 59n, 62,
    66n, 69, 72, 97
Shiubhlaigh, Maire Nic, 29n
Sicilian players, 49, 65
Singing Jail Birds, 96
The Speckled Bird, 17n
Spreading the News, 31, 69
Starkie, Walter, 38n
Symonds, Arthur, 2, 6n, 10, 16n, 81
Synge, John Millington, 38, 39n, 56, 57,
    83, 107
    death, 59n
    influence of Yeats, 17n, 33n, 81

The Tale of a Town, 12n
Theatre of Ireland, 29n, 32
Tillyra Castle, 4, 7n, 18
The Tinker's Wedding, 73, 74n
Tivoli Music Hall, 67
Tobias and the Angel, 30
Tobin, Paddy, 36
Toole, John, 69
Turgenev, Ivan, 11, 13n
Twenty-five, 28, 29n, 64
The Twisting of the Rope, 64
Tyler, George, C., 53

The Untilled Field, 5n

Vale, 7n
Van, Nellie, 76
The Village Schoolmaster, 64

The Wanderings of Usheen, 2
War and Peace, 4
Wilde, Oscar, 40
Wilson, A. Patrick, 86, 87
The Wind Among the Reeds, 2
Wogan Brown girls, 36
The Wooing of Emer, 11, 12
The Workhouse Ward, 25, 42, 46n, 64, 68

Yeats, Jack B., 77, 84n
Yeats, William Butler
    absent from *The Playboy* debut, 41n
    collaborating in writing *Diarmuid*, 6n
    first meeting with Lady Gregory, 16n
    income from poetry, 40
    influence of Lady Gregory, 2, 4, 5, 10,
        14, 17n, 79, 80
    influence on Lady Gregory, 80, 103
    influence on John Synge, 17n, 33n, 81
You Never Can Tell, 36
Young, Arthur, 79